CULTURES OF THE WORLD®

BELGIUM

Robert Pateman & Mark Elliott

MARSHALL CAVENDISH BENCHMARK

NEW YORK

PICTURE CREDITS
Cover photo: © Peter Guttman / CORBIS
AFP: 89, 109 • ANA Press Agency: 97, 127 • Argos: 59, 66, 100, 107, 122 • Bes Stock: 34, 42, 44, 46, 49, 80, 123 • Camera Press: 7, 83 • David Simson: 3, 10, 51, 52, 53, 56, 61, 71, 85, 105, 113, 115, 117 • Eye Ubiquitous / Hutchison: 28, 38, 88, 104 • Focus Team Italy: 6, 20, 40, 43, 50, 70, 84, 103, 108, 110, 124 • HBL Network Photo Agency: 16, 21 • Hulton Deutsch: 18, 22, 24, 30 • Inbel: 33, 57, 77, 119 • International Photobank: 17, 63, 112, 120 • Keith Mundy: 4, 11, 90, 91, 93, 94, 95, 128 • Life File Photos Ltd: 14, 26, 55, 81, 118, 125 • Lonely Planet Images: 58, 102, 126, 129 • Mark De Fraeye: 8, 41, 92, 114 • MCIA — Photodisc: 45 • MCIA — Thomas Khoo & Richard Lee: 131 • National Geographic: 25 • Octavio Iturbe: 99 • Photobank / Photolibrary: 15, 29, 72 • Photolibrary: 111 • Robert Pateman: 60, 62, 68 • Stockfood / FoodPhotogr.Eising: 130 • The Image Bank: 36, 64, 73, 101, 116

PRECEDING PAGE
Two Belgian men in traditional parade costumes.

Editorial Director (U.S.): Michelle Bisson
Editors: Deborah Grahame, Mabelle Yeo, Rizza Manaois
Copyreader: Daphne Hougham
Designers: Jailani Basari, Lock Hong Liang
Cover picture researcher: Connie Gardner
Picture researchers: Thomas Khoo, Joshua Ang

Marshall Cavendish Benchmark
99 White Plains Road
Tarrytown, NY 10591
Web site: www.marshallcavendish.us

© Times Editions Private Limited 1995
© Marshall Cavendish International (Asia) Private Limited 2006
All rights reserved. First edition 1995. Second edition 2006.
® "Cultures of the World" is a registered trademark of Times Publishing Limited.

Originated and designed by Times Editions
An imprint of Marshall Cavendish International (Asia) Private Limited
A member of Times Publishing Limited

All Internet sites were correct and accurate at the time of printing. All monetary figures in this publication are in U.S. dollars.

Library of Congress Cataloging-in-Publication Data
Pateman, Robert, 1954–
　Belgium / by Robert Pateman and Mark Elliott.— 2nd ed.
　　p. cm. — (Cultures of the world)
　Includes bibliographical references and index.
　Summary: "Provides comprehensive information on the geography, history, governmental structure, economy, cultural
　　diversity, peoples, religion, and culture of Belgium" — Provided by publisher.
　　ISBN-13: 978-0-7614-2059-0
　　ISBN-10: 0-7614-2059-2
　1. Belgium—Juvenile literature. I. Elliott, Mark. II. Title. III. Series.
DH418.P38 2006
　949.3—dc22　　　　　　　　　　　2005035839

Printed in China

9 8 7 6 5 4 3 2 1

CONTENTS

Although it is highly industrialized, Belgium is still dotted with farms, many fortified by sturdy outer walls. Many farmyards and some country lanes are still paved with cobbles. This looks old-fashioned, but for animals it makes the surface less slippery than asphalt when conditions get muddy.

3

The Assumption of the Virgin, one of Peter Paul Rubens's masterpieces.

INTRODUCTION

INDEPENDENT SINCE 1830, the Kingdom of Belgium is one of Europe's smallest, wealthiest, and most densely populated countries. It lies at an important crossroads of canals, rivers, railways, and motorways, and Antwerp is one of Europe's most important ports.

Belgium is divided into two very autonomous regions—Flanders in the north, and Wallonia in the south. The language spoken in each region is totally different—a form of French is spoken in Wallonia, while Flemish (a variant of Dutch) is used in Flanders. In both regions people are well educated and predominantly Catholic. However, economic and cultural tensions between the two communities mean that some Flemish favor independence for Flanders. Meanwhile, managing tensions between the two communities means that Belgians tend to be skilled at diplomatic compromise. This is one reason why Belgium has been seen as a model for the multilingual European Union, which has its headquarters in bilingual Brussels, the capital of Belgium.

GEOGRAPHY

COVERING A TOTAL AREA of 11,781 square miles (30,513 square km), Belgium is approximately the same size as Rhode Island and is slightly bigger than Maryland. Even at the widest point, it is only 180 miles (290 km) across. On a map, Belgium's shape resembles a bunch of grapes.

Its important network of canals, rivers, and highways connects the country to eastern and western Europe. The Belgian coastline faces the United Kingdom and the North Sea, one of the world's busiest waterways. The north and northwest parts of the country are low-lying; gently rising plateaus and hilly forests dominate the southern and eastern regions.

Belgium shares borders with the Netherlands to the north, the Grand Duchy of Luxembourg to the southeast, Germany to the east, and France to the south and southwest.

Belgium's only natural boundaries are the 42-mile (68-km) North Sea coastline in the northwest and the Meuse River, that, for a short distance, marks the border between Belgium and the Netherlands.

Left: **The Semois River gently winds through the Ardennes, then enters France, where it joins the Meuse River.**

Opposite: **Plateaus and hilly forests dominate some parts of Belgium.**

The sand dunes along the North Sea coast prevent the sea from flooding the lowlands during high tide.

FERTILE PLAINS AND UNDULATING PLATEAUS

Belgium can be divided into six main regions:

FLANDERS LOWLANDS On the coast of Flanders is a narrow belt of lowlands, reaching from the borders of France to the Schelde River. The area has many fine sandy beaches and dunes. Behind the dunes lie the *polders* (POHL-duhrs), land reclaimed from the sea and protected from floods by the natural barrier of dunes and artificial sea walls. The *polders* are formed by thin, sandy soil overlying clay and require heavy fertilization before they can be farmed.

Inland, the plains of Flanders extend southwest and are crossed by the Leie, Schelde, and Dender rivers. Intensive farming and industrial development characterize this area.

THE CENTRAL LOW PLATEAU The plateau rises to a height of 700 feet (213 m) in the south. It includes Belgium's best farmland, the result of the region's rich alluvial soils.

The Senne, Demer, and Dijle rivers cross the plateau toward the Rupel River, ending in the Schelde River. Once covered with forests, the landscape has long been transformed by dense human habitation. Light industry is common along the region's impressive road network. While farmlands dotted with villages are a familiar sight, these increasingly merge into one another along major roads. Brussels, the capital of Belgium, lies at the center of this region.

THE KEMPENLAND PLATEAU In the north, by the Dutch border and between the Schelde and Meuse rivers, rich farmland gives way to a region of sand dunes, scrub moorland, and coniferous forest. Just as in the south, coal deposits are mined in the region.

The Kempenland is now a light-industrial district. The region also has an atomic research and nuclear power center, a recycling plant, and a large army base. Cutting through pleasant wooded countryside, the Albert Canal, which links the Meuse and Schelde rivers, carries barge traffic on the way to Antwerp. Modern roads connect the region to Belgium's major cities and to Germany's industrialized Ruhr Valley.

THE SAMBRE-MEUSE VALLEY This narrow but well-defined region is approximately 100 miles (161 km) long, but it is only about 3 to 10 miles (5 to 16 km) wide. Extending from the south to the north of Belgium along the Sambre and Meuse rivers, the valley connects the central low plateau to the higher plateau of the Ardennes region. Coal mining used to be the main industry here, and it had supported other heavy industries; thus this region became one of the most populated in Belgium.

THE ARDENNES This plateau lies east of the Sambre-Meuse Valley. This was once a large mountain range, but the mountaintops were long ago worn down by glaciers. Today the Ardennes region consists largely of sandstone ridges, limestone valleys, and woodland hills rising above 1,000 feet (305 m). Close to the German border are some high hills: the Botrange is the highest point at 2,277 feet (694 m), and the Baraque Michel rises to 2,111 feet (643 m). The Ardennes region has excellent hiking trails, fast-flowing rivers, and winter snow, making it a major recreational area.

Several distinctive subareas have their own geographical names. Hilly Hageland, east of Leuven, is famous for fruit and produces a variety of wines. The Borinage is the industrialized former coal mining zone around Mons. The Ostkantonen are pretty German-speaking areas close to Eupen. Westhoek, in far western Flanders, consists of the flat fields made infamous by World War I.

BELGIAN LORRAINE This region, located at the extreme southeastern point of the country, rises to more than 1,300 feet (396 m). Part of the Paris Basin, soils here are far more fertile than in the bordering Ardennes. Farming and agriculture are the main occupations. Some iron deposits support steel mills and other industries, but this has not stopped the migration of its population to the cities.

CLIMATE

Belgium has a reasonably gentle maritime climate due to prevailing winds from the west, which are warmed by the vast expanse of the Atlantic Ocean. Generally, summers are comfortably warm at around 70°F (21°C) without becoming overly hot. Winters are cold but seldom severe, with temperatures usually varying between 37°F (3°C) and 52°F (11°C).

Although the weather is usually mild, there are long periods of dull, gray days with abundant rain. Fog is common. Rainfall is rarely very heavy,

The area south of Namur city in the Sambre-Meuse Valley has many fascinating caves rich in stalactites and dramatic rock formations. Some of the caves have rivers flowing through them and have been opened to tourists.

RIVERS

Belgium's river and canal system has played an important role in shaping the country's economy.

The Meuse (Maas in Flemish) is a gently flowing river that starts in eastern France and runs north into Belgium. It has cut a steep, narrow valley through the Ardennes, and it flows past the canyon town of Dinant before the Sambre joins it at the fortress city of Namur.

The Meuse continues to flow north, collecting other rivers as it goes. It runs into the Netherlands, and from there enters the sea south of Rotterdam. The Meuse is nearly 600 miles (965 km) long, and ships can sail up and down much of this length. Where the river is too shallow to allow ships to pass, canals have been cut. Of all the navigable rivers in Europe, only the Rhine is more important.

The Schelde (l'Escault in French) is 270 miles (434 km) long and is a vital link in the European transportation network. The river starts in northern France and flows past Ghent (Gent), where it is joined by the Leie River. It then takes a northeasterly direction, eventually reaching Antwerp, which is Europe's second biggest port, despite being some 55 miles (88 km) inland. The building of new locks has enabled the harbor facilities to extend another 8 miles (13 km) downriver. (A lock is a portion of a canal with gates at either end, the closing and opening of which adjusts the water level in that part of the canal.) Over 15,000 ships dock in Antwerp every year: that is more than 40 every day. Although this number is around 10 percent fewer than 30 years ago, ships are now much bigger and almost three times heavier than before.

but light rain can fall constantly for lengthy periods. When occasional winds blow from the east, across the Eurasian landmass, they bring more severe weather: snow, storms, and periods of unusual cold in winter or heat waves in summer.

The hilly terrain of the Ardennes tends to be generally cooler and receives much more rain and snow than other areas. Only the summer months, from May to early October, are free of frost. Usually the area has heavy winter snows.

The warming influence of the sea makes coastal areas somewhat drier and sunnier than inland regions. Ostend, on the Belgian coast, averages about 1,760 hours of sunshine each year, while Brussels, less than 100 miles (161 km) away, gets around 1,585 hours.

In recent years global warming has resulted in hotter summers, colder winters, and a more tropical variety of rainfall, which increases the risks of flooding.

FLORA AND FAUNA

In the past Belgium was covered with deciduous forests. Oak was the most common tree, but beech, birch, and elm also thrived. Over the centuries, much of the original forest has been cleared for farmland or housing. The country's wildlife has been greatly affected by the destruction of the forests, but the forested Ardennes region is still a major refuge for animals such as boars, red deer, wildcats, and tree martens. The coastal region has its own rich fauna. This area is a vital resting ground for migrating birds and a winter home for many northern birds.

Belgium has 17 nature reserves and national parks. The Hautes Fagnes Nature Park, by far the largest, covers 167,655 acres (67,850 ha) of boggy fenland east of the Ardennes. The much smaller Lesse and Lomme Park is Belgium's oldest reserve, protecting a beautiful stretch of Ardennes riverside. On the coast toward the Dutch border, the Zwin Nature Reserve covers a tidal wetland area that is important for over a hundred different species of birds as well as the unique dune vegetation. Farther south, the Westhoek Nature Reserve has been set up to protect about 840 acres (340 h) of sand dunes. As building continues along the coast, this might soon be the last area to retain the coast's original appearance. Despite these efforts, much of Belgium's wildlife, including some bat species and many wild plants, are still endangered.

CITIES

BRUSSELS (Brussel in Flemish, Bruxelles in French) is the capital of Belgium. The region includes 19 communes (boroughs) of which one is the central, historical City of Brussels (also incorporating Laeken and the "European Quarter"). The whole Brussels metropolitan area spreads into several Flemish towns, including Vilvoorde and Zaventenm where the international airport is located.

Brussels is at the hub of Belgium's roadway and rail networks. It is the headquarters of many international organizations, including NATO and the European Union. Its major industries include mechanical engineering, food processing, textiles, chemicals, electronics, and printing. Construction work is also very important, and there are several major international corporate headquarters in the suburban fields and forests just beyond the official city limits.

ANTWERP (Antwerpen in Flemish, Anvers in French) is Belgium's second largest city. It is the fifth busiest port in the world and, after Rotterdam in the Netherlands, the second busiest in Europe. In addition to being an important industrial city, Antwerp is also a major diamond center: 40 percent of the world's cutting and 70 percent of the polishing are conducted there.

LIÈGE (Luik in Flemish) stands where the Meuse and Ourthe rivers meet. It is Belgium's third largest city and was the site of the country's first coal mine. It was developed early as a commercial, financial, and industrial center. Various wars and battles over the years have destroyed much of the old city.

GHENT (Gent in Flemish, Gand in French) was a Roman city that grew into a great trading center during the Middle Ages. Magnificent buildings

MANNEKEN PIS

The Manneken Pis has become the semiofficial symbol of Brussels, and it fits well with the citizens' gentle, self-mocking humor. He even has his own Web site (www.manneken-pis.com). Nobody really knows why the statue was built, but there are numerous far-fetched tales of its origin.

One version is that an unknown boy made the mistake of relieving himself outside a witch's house. The angry witch responded by turning him into a statue. In another story the statue was put up by grateful parents whose son was found on this spot after wandering off during a busy carnival. More common than either of those is the tale of a little boy who spotted a fire during his excursion to the outhouse one evening. By raising the alarm, he saved the city from being burned down.

Manneken Pis was originally a stone statue, carved by Jérôme Duquesnoy in 1619. It was replaced by a bronze version in 1817. Both suffered frequent thefts by student pranksters and by invading armies. Troops of Louis XV stole one in 1747 and dumped it outside a brothel. The French king apologized by sending a fine set of clothes to "dress" him. Since then, Manneken Pis's wardrobe has grown to over 650 garments. He often wears uniforms or national costumes depending on sponsors and special occasions.

The name Antwerpen *is a combination of the words* hand *(hand) and* werpen *(to throw).*

of that time still stand, including the town hall, cathedral, belfry, and cloth hall. Much of Ghent's charm and character comes from the many branches of the Schelde and Leie rivers that flow through the town. Ghent is also a thriving modern city, with a steelworks and factories that produce paper, chemicals, cars, and electrical goods. Although it is over 20 miles (32 km) from the sea, Ghent is linked to the coast by a canal and has its own harbor.

BRUGES (Brugge in Flemish) is sometimes called the Venice of the North because of its beautiful canals, bridges, monuments, and buildings—some of them dating from the 15th and 16th centuries. The city was once one of the greatest commercial cities in Europe. Today it is a major tourist town, but there are also breweries and other industries. Bruges is linked by a canal with the port of Zeebrugge about 7 miles (11 km) to the west.

MONS (Bergen in Flemish) was a wealthy trading city that suffered considerable bombing in World War II but remains colorful and appealing. It is especially boisterous during its Saint Wadru festival. Mons is the headquarters of SHAPE (Supreme Headquarters Allied Powers Europe), the military command center for NATO in Europe.

LEUVEN (Louvain in French) was an important center of the medieval cloth industry and has one of the world's most ornate city hall buildings. It is the home of one of Europe's oldest universities, founded in 1425.

NAMUR (Namen in Flemish) was historically one of Europe's most heavily defended citadels. The quiet city is now the capital of Wallonia, Belgium's French-speaking region.

CHARLEROI is the heartland of Belgium's Italian community. It is economically depressed due to the decline of its traditional mining and steel industries.

MECHELEN (Malines in French) was once a powerful religious and cultural city famous for lace making. Today its focus is on furniture making and light industry. After its ongoing face-lift, it is likely to grow in importance as a tourist center.

OSTEND (Oostende in Flemish, Ostende in French) is Belgium's biggest coastal town and its main fishing and ferry port. The town commands a long stretch of sandy beaches that is popular with local vacationers.

According to a Flemish legend, a giant would chop off the hands of any sailor who did not pay a toll when sailing into Antwerp harbor. The severed hands were thrown into the Schelde River. He was stopped by a Roman soldier, Silvius Brabo, who cut the giant's hands off. Brabo's statue now stands on Antwerp's main square.

HISTORY

ARCHAEOLOGICAL FINDS REVEAL that various tribes had been living in what is now Belgium for thousands of years. By 2000 B.C. Celtic tribes had settled in Belgium where they intermarried with Germanic tribes from northern Netherlands.

ROMAN RULE

In 52 B.C. Julius Caesar and his Roman army conquered the area between the Seine and Rhine rivers. They had fought a fierce battle against a tribe of people known as the Belgae, which Caesar described as being the bravest of all the Gauls. The Belgae would give their name to Belgium many centuries later.

Under the Romans, Belgium became a rich trading center, and in time most people adopted Roman customs. The towns of Tournai and Tongeren grew to be the most important Roman cities in the region. They each had a big army camp, and strong walls surrounded the cities to protect them against foreign invaders.

The Romans stayed for nearly 500 years, but as Roman power declined, tribes of Franks from central Europe settled in the marshy lands to the north of the country. In A.D. 496 Clovis I, king of the Franks, defeated the Romans. The Franks spoke a Germanic language, different from the Romanized speech of the south, so that even at this early date the inhabitants of future-Belgium were divided into two language groups.

Christianity was first taken to Belgium at this time by Irish and Scottish missionaries. They converted Clovis, but it was a second wave of Christianity in the seventh century that had more impact. It was at this time that many of Belgium's great monasteries were founded.

Above: **Ghent's medieval castle, Gravensteen, is surrounded by thick walls and water to repel invasions.**

Opposite: **Statue of Godfrey of Bouillon, a Belgian noble who led and partly financed the first crusade.**

Even before his death, Charlemagne's brilliant efforts and achievements made him a legendary figure and the subject of veneration in churches. His image is portrayed in Belgium's earliest epic poems and written stories.

FROM TURMOIL TO TRADE

Between A.D. 768 and 814 much of Europe was united under the powerful King Charlemagne and the Belgian area became a very important and prosperous part of the Holy Roman Empire, the medieval state that embraced most of Central Europe. Being a great organizer, Charlemagne built roads and developed the existing waterways. He promoted intellectual life and the arts.

When Charlemagne died in 814, his kingdom disintegrated and his sons divided their father's empire between France and Lotharingia. The region became more feudalized, and coastal areas suffered the raids of fierce Viking warriors from the north. Nobles lived in fortified castles, and towns built strong walls for protection.

Local counts and dukes grew more and more powerful and independent and became a major force in European politics. When the crusaders strode off to war against the Muslim rulers of Jerusalem, many present-day Belgian nobles gathered their armies and marched with them. Godfrey of Bouillon was one of the leaders at the siege of Jerusalem and was awarded the title "Steward and Protector of the Holy Sepulchre."

From the 12th century onward, Flanders (northern Belgium) started to grow rich from its cloth trade. Flemish cloth was flexible, colorful, and soft. It was popular with rich and noble families throughout Europe. Flanders was soon using more wool than it could produce, and merchants traveled to Britain to buy more. Towns such as Ypres (Ieper), Ghent (Gent), and Bruges (Brugge) became great trading centers. They sold cloth and metal from south Belgium and bought wool, grain, smoked fish, furs, and timber from all over Europe. Soon the trading activities were regulated by strong guilds. As the merchants became wealthier, they were able to bargain for political rights through charters for their towns and increased their independence.

BATTLE OF THE GOLDEN SPURS

The Battle of the Golden Spurs, which took place over 600 years ago, occupies an important place in Flemish history. In 1214 King Philip II of France defeated the Flemish and their English allies at the Battle of Bouvines, taking partial control of Flanders. Over the next hundred years the French became more powerful in Flanders and, by the 1300s, seemed ready to annex the land and make it part of France.

However, on the night of May 18, 1302, the citizens of Bruges rebelled, overpowering the guard and murdering everybody they suspected of being French. Encouraged by this news, ordinary people from all over Flanders gathered at Kortrijk (Courtrai) on July 11. The French knights were better-armed, but the better-motivated Flemish people eventually defeated them and saved Flanders from French occupation, although only for a short time. The battle became known as the Battle of the Golden Spurs because afterward the Flemings gathered more than 700 golden spurs from dead French noblemen. May 18 is still commemorated as the National Day of Flanders.

THE BURGUNDIAN PERIOD

Despite relative prosperity, times were still uncertain. Periods of bad weather could bring famines, there was almost continuous warfare, and terrible plagues struck the population, killing thousands of people. During these periods of unrest and calamity the dukes of Burgundy, who were rich and influential noblemen, rose to power in the region. By the early 15th century they ruled over the 17 provinces that today make up most of Belgium and the Netherlands.

Duke Philip the Good is the most famous of the Burgundian rulers. He reigned from 1419 to 1467, extending his domain in battle and improving the economy by reforming tax laws, banning English cloth, and promoting the Antwerp trade fairs.

As the free citizens grew more powerful through trade, they helped pay for the great town halls that are still admired in so many cities today. Rich merchants, the nobility, and the church started to invest their money in art, and a golden age of Flemish painters developed.

The 14th and 15th centuries saw some cities decline and others prosper. Brussels grew into the regional capital for the province of Brabant. The dukes of Burgundy occasionally held court there, which furthered the growth of the city. The Zwin, an estuary that formed Bruges's access to the sea, silted up, and the city slowly declined. This allowed Antwerp to emerge as a new and dynamic trading center.

The medieval glory of Bruges is still evident in the old guildhalls and merchants' houses and the small canals that once linked the city with the North Sea.

SPANISH RULE

When Philip's son, Charles the Bold, was killed in battle in 1477, his daughter Mary married Maximilian of Austria, which brought Burgundian lands under the control of the Germanic Hapsburg family. The Hapsburgs were related to nearly all the royal families in Europe, and under Maximilian's grandson, King Charles V of Spain, present-day Belgium and the northeastern Netherlands became part of the powerful Spanish empire. It was one of the greatest empires Europe had seen since Roman times.

Cultural differences, however, were growing considerably. In the north, prosperity and education meant that many people had learned to read. The development of printing enabled local Christians to read the Bible for themselves instead of learning about Christianity from priests who were often corrupt. The result was Protestantism—a new form of Christianity that rapidly became popular in northern Germany and the Netherlands, including Belgium. When Charles V's Roman Catholic son, Philip, came to power, he saw Protestantism as a major evil. This led to 30 years of war. Initially, the Netherlands, including much of present-day Belgium, broke away from Spanish rule and set up its own independent nation. Spain eventually recaptured the area that is now Belgium (then known as the Spanish Netherlands). The people suffered considerable religious persecution. As part of peace negotiations with Holland, Antwerp, one of Europe's greatest port cities, was closed to trade. This created great economic problems for Belgium, which was left as a forgotten corner of the Spanish empire.

A massive carpet of flowers covers the Grand Place square in Brussels as part of a tourist attraction. The Grand Place was the target of French bombardment in 1695. The medieval grandeur of guildhalls, with their gilded scrollwork and statues, was restored in a curious mixture of French and Italian Renaissance styles.

In 1659 King Louis XIV assumed power in France. He was determined to make the Spanish Netherlands part of his kingdom. The Spanish Netherlands became a battleground between the French and the newly independent Dutch, often aided by other European powers. In 1695 the French surrounded and bombarded Brussels, destroying much of the ancient city. However, a series of campaigns led by Britain's duke of Marlborough and Prince Eugène of Savoy finally forced the French out of the region.

In the Treaty of Utrecht, France abandoned any claim to the Spanish Netherlands. The European powers, however, were uncertain as to what to do with the area. They did not think it could survive as an independent nation. As a result, Spanish Netherlands was given to Charles VI, the emperor of Austria, and the area became known as the Austrian Netherlands.

21

THE BATTLE OF WATERLOO

After a series of defeats in 1813 and 1814, France's emperor and master general, Napoleon Bonaparte, was exiled to the island of Elba off the coast of Italy. In 1815 he escaped and, incredibly, swiftly regained power in France. A coalition of armies was assembled against him, and Napoleon knew that he had to strike first to knock them out before more could arrive.

On June 16, 1815, he hit first at the Prussian army at Ligny. Thinking that they were defeated, he then marched against his old foe, the British duke of Wellington. Wellington cunningly moved back to a more defendable position just south of Waterloo village. There, behind a hedgerow atop a gentle ridge, he deployed his 200,000-strong force of English, Flemish, and Dutch troops with over 400 cannons.

Heavy rain delayed and confused Napoleon's attack plan. Hours later the French struck at Wellington's right flank. This was not supposed to be the main attack, but more and more soldiers were drawn into the battle. In the early afternoon Napoleon finally launched his main assault on the center of the allied line.

As the afternoon wore on, despite a desperate attack by Napoleon's elite Old Guard, the allied line held firm. Then, much to Napoleon's surprise, he found the Prussian army arriving to attack the French flank. They had not retreated after their earlier defeat, but were now coming to Wellington's assistance. As more and more Prussian forces appeared, French hopes faded. Their weary army started to break up and flee south, and Napoleon himself was very nearly captured. Napoleon, who had previously revolutionized warfare, had here waged a strangely unimaginative battle.

THE FIGHT FOR INDEPENDENCE

The 1789 Brabant Revolution briefly declared independence for the Belgian provinces of the Austrian Netherlands and established the United States of Belgium, which was later suppressed in 1790 by the Austrians.

In 1794 the Austrian Netherlands was suddenly conquered by France's new revolutionary government. French rule, under Emperor Napoleon Bonaparte, brought many important modernizing reforms. Industry was encouraged and the port of Antwerp, closed for many years, was reopened. The metric system and a new legal code were introduced, and Belgium was divided into nine departments.

However, the French were never popular, and their defeat in 1814 was generally welcomed. A few months later Napoleon once again marched into Belgium, only to meet his defeat at the Battle of Waterloo in June 1815. Some 54,000 men died in that battle, which was one of the bloodiest and most decisive in European history.

At the Congress of Vienna in June 1815, the European powers reorganized Europe. They particularly wanted to prevent France from further expansion and from ever gaining control of the port of Antwerp. Under the influence of Great Britain, the Congress united the area with the Netherlands under the reign of William of Orange. However, in August 1830 a revolution broke out against Dutch rule, and by the end of the year, Belgium had declared independence.

Belgium's new constitution was considered dangerously progressive for the era. To counterbalance this liberalism, the founding fathers decided to look for a constitutional monarch. Several candidates declined. Eventually, German Prince Leopold of Saxe-Coburg-Gotha, an uncle of Britain's Queen Victoria, received the final approval of the major European powers. King Leopold I ascended the throne on July 21, 1831, the date now recognized as Belgium's National Day.

INDUSTRY AND COLONY

Few observers in 1831 really expected this artificial country to last more than a decade. However, King Leopold proved to be an able statesman and the economy prospered. Europe was being transformed by the Industrial Revolution and Belgium was in the ideal position to benefit from such industrialization. The newly independent nation had excellent harbors, both on the coast and inland, and seemingly endless coal fields. In 1835 the first railway line on the mainland of Europe was opened between

Mechelen and Brussels. Equally important, Belgium's neutrality seemed to be accepted.

Leopold II ascended to the throne in 1865. He believed that to finance Belgium's further development as a modern European nation and to raise the prestige of the country and the royal court, it should become a colonial power. He commissioned British explorer Henry Stanley to make a second trip to central Africa, carrying treaties of loyalty to the Belgian king. While there, Stanley persuaded many local chieftains to sign the treaties, effectively seceding sovereignty over their land to Leopold and allowing him to establish the Congo Free State (now the Democratic Republic of Congo), which he proceeded to rule as his personal property.

In the 19th century controversial King Leopold II funded Brussels's transformation into an elegant modern city using income gained by the sweat and toil of the Congolese people in his vast, resource-rich African colony.

The territory yielded rubber, ivory, and other valuable resources, making the king wealthy enough to develop Belgian industry and to construct many great buildings, turning Brussels into a fashionable European capital. This was achieved at the cost of virtual slavery for the Congolese people, however, who suffered and often died under appalling conditions of forced labor. There were international protests against the treatment of the population. In 1908 the Belgian government was forced to take over the colony.

THE VIOLENT CENTURY

For much of the 19th century Belgium lived under the shadow of its powerful neighbor France. By the beginning of the 20th century it was Germany, newly emerged as a united nation, that gave greater concern. In August 1914 German troops marched across Belgian soil to attack France, plunging Belgium into World War I. The tiny Belgian army put up a brave fight and even flooded some areas of their countryside to slow down the Germans while British and French troops were rushed in to help. By October 1914 the German advance was halted. Only a tiny corner of northwest Belgium remained unoccupied but the Belgian king, Albert I, refused to leave it. (Today, Albert is still considered a hero. He is commonly depicted in statues wearing a simple soldier's helmet.)

Both sides dug a line of trenches that stretched from the Belgian coast through France and on to the Swiss border. Neither side could break through this defense system, and the war dragged on from one year to the next. It was a time of great hardship for the Belgians, most of whom were trapped in German-occupied territory.

The Great War of 1914 to 1918 (World War I), some of which was fought on Belgian soil, cost millions of lives on both sides without achieving victory for either. The Belgian cities of Ieper and Diksmuide and villages close to the front line were totally destroyed. It was 1918 before the arrival of large numbers of U.S. troops did finally help bring about the Allied victory.

A memorial for the dead of Word War I.

After the war the right to vote was extended to all Belgian men; woman suffrage was granted only in 1948. The new government introduced major social reforms that included reducing the working day to eight hours, reforming taxes, and introducing old-age insurance. Although these changes helped to improve the standard of living for the majority of people, the worldwide Great Depression of 1929 to 1939 caused considerable hardship and poverty. The 1930s also brought new political tensions, with the rise of Hitler and the Nazi party in Germany.

In May 1940 Belgians woke to find that once again their country had been invaded by the German army. Using tanks and aircraft, the Germans were able to overrun the whole of Belgium in only 18 days. This time the

The Atomium was built in 1958 for a world's fair. Representing the atomic-crystal structure of iron, it has become a Brussels landmark, and it was completely renovated in 2005.

occupying army was to stay for five years, and in many ways the occupation was even more brutal and devastating than in World War I. Many Belgians were sent to Germany to work as forced laborers, and the Jewish population suffered unimaginable persecution.

In Belgium the population had to deal with several problems: a freeze in wages, high inflation, a rationed food supply, and a flourishing black market. The Germans fought resistance operations and bombings with violent counterterrorist activities and reprisals.

For Belgium, World War II was a time of great confusion. In contrast to King Albert in World War I, King Leopold III quickly surrendered to the Germans. Although the king stayed in occupied Belgium, the Belgian government fled and set up a government-in-exile in London in October 1940. Belgian troops based there continued to fight alongside the Allies.

The Allies invaded northern France on June 6, 1944, D-Day, and by September had liberated most of Belgium. However, Hitler launched a last desperate counterattack at Christmas 1944 in the Ardennes region. The American 101st Airborne Division was surrounded in the small town of Bastogne. When the Germans demanded their surrender, commander General McCauliffe famously responded curtly with a single word: "Nuts." The Americans fought bravely, losing almost 80,000 troops in combat. After many more battles the Germans in Belgium were finally defeated by the end of January 1945. Bastogne, grateful to the American troops, renamed its central square Place McCauliffe.

POSTWAR RECOVERY AND RECENT HISTORY

The postwar economy flourished, and Belgium became a founding member of the European Economic Community (now the European Union). Social

INDEPENDENCE IN AFRICA

After World War II, Belgium was reluctant to let go of its African colonies, the Belgian Congo and the Belgian-administered trust territory of Ruanda-Urundi. However, a changing world order and increasing resistance in the colonies eventually made their independence inevitable.

The Congo gained its independence on June 30, 1960. With its great wealth of natural resources, it was hoped that the young nation would become a major African power. Instead, tribal conflicts broke out, and the rich mining province of Katanga tried to break away as an independent state. The country became involved in a bitter civil war, and many Belgian citizens who had hoped to stay in Africa were forced to leave.

Western governments put their hopes and support behind Congo's president Mobutu Sese Seko. At first he did bring some political stability to the nation whose name he changed to Zaire. But over the years, Zaire became more and more corrupt. While the government failed to provide its people with basic services, the president and his family became notorious for their personal wealth, which ran to over four billion dollars. After the end of the cold war and the USSR's collapse in 1991, the West no longer wanted to support corrupt Mobutu, and Zaire virtually collapsed. Belgian troops were sent to help evacuate an estimated 11,000 Belgian citizens from the trouble-torn country as a civil war threatened to destroy the nation. Mobutu fled in 1997, and the country was renamed the Democratic Republic of Congo, although democracy as yet remains more an idea than a reality.

Belgium took over Ruanda-Urundi from Germany during World War I. In 1962 it was split into two small, independent nations, Burundi and Rwanda. Each country had for centuries been dominated by the Tutsi tribe, even though ethnic Hutu people were the larger majority. In both countries cycles of violence followed the first democratic elections, in which the Hutus gained a majority. In Rwanda the result was a settling of scores culminating in the infamous genocide of 1994, including the murder of ten Belgian peacekeepers. In Burundi the first Hutu president was assassinated by Tutsis and a decade of civil war has rumbled on ever since, killing around 300,000.

conditions improved but simmering differences between the major linguistic groups culminated in serious riots in 1968. To defuse tensions, the Flemish-, French-, and German-speaking communities were given responsibilities over their own educational and cultural affairs.

After a period of stagnation in the 1970s, the economy rebounded in the 1980s. However, economic growth proved much stronger in Flanders than in Wallonia where heavy industries remained moribund. This disparity fueled continuing north-south linguistic conflicts that led eventually to federalism. A revised 1993 constitution divided Belgium into three highly autonomous regions: Flanders, Wallonia, and Brussels-Capital Region. In 2005 Belgium celebrated its 175th anniversary.

GOVERNMENT

BELGIUM IS A CONSTITUTIONAL MONARCHY. Since 1993, real power has been divided between three national and regional authorities: the national government, the regions, and the linguistic communities. Each administrative level has exclusive powers within its mandate and does not interfere with the other authorities, although their territories geographically overlap. There are also two levels of local government: provinces and communes.

NATIONAL GOVERNMENT

Although the king is the official head of state, Belgium is ruled by national parliament, which has responsibility for foreign policy, the national economy, justice, and defense. The Parliament consists of two houses. New bills, which make the nation's laws, have to be passed by both houses. However, the elected 150-member Chamber of Representatives is generally the major force. The 71-seat Senate is generally more concerned with longer-term legislation and constitutional matters.

The Senate's composition is rather complex: 41 members must be Flemish speaking, 29 Francophone, and one appointed German-speaking senator. Of these, one Flemish speaker and six French speakers must live in Brussels-Capital Region. Only 40 members are elected by the public, according to a territorially defined system of electoral colleges. Another 21 members are assigned by community councils. The last 10 members are co-opted by the other senators. Curiously, the monarch's children are entitled to be extra senators once they are over 18 years of age.

Elections for both houses are held at the same time and must be conducted at least every four years. As Belgian governments are complex coalitions of multiple parties, it is not unusual for the term to actually be shorter. All Belgians over the age of 18 have the right to vote and are required to do so by law.

Above: **The Belgian flag has three vertical stripes in red, yellow, and black. The shape is unusually square. On the right is the blue European Union flag with a ring of yellow stars.**

Opposite: **The European Parliament has three places of work—in Brussels, Luxembourg, and Strasbourg.**

The Belgian Parliament meets in these chambers.

POLITICAL PARTIES

There are currently 23 main political parties in Belgium. Votes are by proportional representation with a minimum quota, so not all parties make it into Parliament, while others form multiparty umbrella groups to ensure a degree of mutual success. Parties relatively frequently change names and composition, and form alliances with other parties. However, in reality most parties fall into one of three main groupings—Christian, Socialist, and Liberal. Within each category there are yet different parties for French and Flemish speakers.

The Christian groups, including Flemish Christian-Democratic and Flemish (CD&V) and Francophone Humanist Democratic Centre (CDH) tend to take conservative center-right, status-quo positions, though by U.S. standards, they would be seen as quite liberal. As a previous incarnation called the Christian People's Party (CVP), the CD&V had for years been the strongest party in Flanders and was the party of former prime ministers Wilfred Martens and Jean-Luc Dehaene. The party of the prime minister in 2006, Guy Verhofstadt, represents the Flemish Liberal Democrats (VLD). Their Francophone equivalent is the Reformist Movement (MR) an umbrella party combining Party of Reform and Liberty (PRL), Democratic Front of Francophones (FDF), Citizens' Movement for Change (MCC) and Party for Freedom and Progress (PFF), which the Minister of Finances, Didier Reynders, represents. The Socialist parties typically concentrate on social welfare issues, and the Francophone Socialists (PS) is the leading party in Wallonia. PS member André Flahaut is currently the Minister of Defense. The extreme complexity of the current coalition serves, to some extent, to prevent the extreme right-wing Flemish nationalist Vlaams Belang party from getting into power.

Vlaams Belang was created when the former Vlams Blok was declared to be a racist party. Both have called for the expulsion of immigrants, but may probably attract votes because people feel that voting for them is one way to demonstrate their discontentment with a status quo where eternal compromises mean that little appears to get done. The ecological parties—ECOLO in Wallonia and Groen (formerly AGALEV) in Flanders were part of the ruling coalition until 2003.

REGIONS AND COMMUNITIES

Since the November 1995 elections, Flanders, Wallonia, and Brussels-Capital each elects a regional parliament and a minister-president. These regional parliaments take responsibility for planning infrastructure, water, energy, regional road development, and tourism within their areas. Each is highly autonomous. Although technically all foreign policy is decided at a national level, Flanders also sends its own representatives to many countries. The Wallonia Parliament meets in Namur, but Flanders has established its seat of government in Brussels.

The country is also divided into three "Communities," responsible for cultural matters, broadcasting, education, and health. These also have their own parliaments or councils, though the parliaments of the Flemish-speaking community (Vlaamse Gemeenschap) and of Flanders are de facto merged into one. The French-speaking Community (Communauté Francaise) covers most of Wallonia, including French-speaking institutions in bilingual Brussels, where it is based. The German-speaking Community (Deutschsprachige Gemeinschaft) encompasses roughly 70,000 people in Wallonia's eastern cantons around Eupen and has a council rather than a parliament.

There are nearly 13,000 councillors in Belgium, meaning that one in every 600 people is directly involved in local politics. Most of these councillors are part-time politicians who carry out council business in their spare time.

Incredibly, Brussels is home to no fewer than five different parliaments: those of Belgium, the European Union, the Brussels-Capital Region, Flanders (combined with that of the Flemish Community), and the Francophone Community.

REGIONAL AND LOCAL POLITICS

Belgium is divided into 10 provinces. Flanders and Wallonia have five provinces each. Although every province has its own directly elected provincial council and a governor appointed by the king, these have relatively minor political power compared with the regions or the much smaller municipalities and municipal boroughs. Most Belgians have a strong historical sense of local autonomy, and each of Belgium's 589 municipalities has a great deal of authority. Each commune has its own elected council and mayor, known as *burgemeester* in Flemish, *bourgemestre* in Belgian French. The *bourgemestre* is appointed by the king on the advice of the municipal council. It is not uncommon for high profile mayors to also become ministers or national politicians at the same time. When this occurs, the actual day-to-day mayoral tasks are frequently delegated to city aldermen. Aldermen are elected by the borough council from among their own members.

The municipality is responsible for most matters of local interest, including the budget, utility rates, weddings, garbage collection, and the issuing of drivers' licenses. Until recently they even issued passports, but this has now been centralized to improve security.

THE EUROPEAN UNION

Brussels is the home of the European Union (EU), which is becoming an increasingly powerful force in European politics. The EU was born in 1958 with just six member nations and at first aimed simply to remove trade tariffs within Europe and create a common market. Now it has grown to 25 members and is bringing the nations of Europe closer in many different areas. One major goal is to spread wealth and investment to help new member nations improve their prosperity and thereby gain stability.

At present most of the important agreements and decisions are made by the Council of Ministers. EU members are usually the foreign ministers of the

SOVEREIGN POWER

King Baudouin died suddenly in July 1993, after ruling for 42 years. He often acted as a mediator between the two major language groups and enjoyed overwhelming popularity. Because King Baudouin and his wife were childless, Baudouin's brother became King Albert II. Along with Queen Paola (in photo with King Albert), the king is well liked for his easy, relatively unpretentious style. The royal couple has three children, including heir to the throne Prince Philippe.

The king of Belgium has many roles. He is the commander-in-chief of the armed forces, appoints and dismisses ministers, convenes or dissolves parliament, confirms and signs the new laws, and is involved in the selection and appointment of judges and senior diplomats. Most of these roles are symbolic.

Although his actual monarchical power is strictly controlled today, the king exerts considerable influence. He can be an impartial arbiter in disputes and has almost daily contact with high management and decision-making people in all realms of Belgian life. The king has to sign the laws and cannot really refuse. In April 1990 the country faced a brief constitutional crisis when the devoutly Catholic King Baudouin felt he could not sign the government's new abortion laws. To solve the problem, the king temporarily abdicated from the throne for 36 hours. His brother, acting as temporary monarch, approved the laws. After that was done, Baudouin resumed his position.

member nations, but meetings might involve other ministers, depending on the agenda. Usually the heads of governments meet once or twice a year for a European Council. Decisions reached at these meetings are passed to the European Commission. The commission is the EU executive body, made up of professional bureaucrats selected by a long series of public examinations. It is nicknamed the Eurocracy and—given the 20 official languages—the teams of secretaries, translators, and accountants are very large. They attempt to develop common standards for member nations on a wide range of issues from beach pollution to standards for drinking water.

Although there is an elected European Parliament, this does not yet have the powers normally associated with parliaments and cannot make laws. Its influence is really limited to posing questions to both the European Commission and the Council of Ministers.

ECONOMY

BELGIUM IS ONE OF THE WEALTHIEST countries in the world. It enjoys low inflation, and its industries are increasingly modern and competitive despite intense global competition. The population is well educated and the workforce is one of the most productive in the world. Belgium is proud of having a high quality-of-life index and an excellent social system, which means that there are relatively few genuinely poor or homeless people, contrary to the situation in many more strictly capitalist nations. Nonetheless, as with most socially generous countries, Belgium is facing some serious economic strains. Unemployment remains a problem, and although good government has balanced the books, a large budget deficit remains. In October 2005 highly unpopular attempts to save money by changing the pensions and social security systems resulted in a national one-day strike, the first such strike in 12 years.

Being a small country, Belgium has a limited domestic market, and firms need to sell their goods overseas. Two out of every three of Belgium's industrial workers produce goods for export, and the country exports about 120 million dollars' worth of commodities and services daily. This reliance on exports means that the Belgian economy can be seriously affected by international events. Belgium's main trading partners are France, Germany, the Netherlands, Great Britain, and the United States.

INDUSTRY

Industry now employs less than 25 percent of the labor force. Much of present-day industry involves importing raw materials and exporting finished or semifinished goods. The range of Belgian products is quite remarkable and includes cars, locomotives, textiles, plastics, glass, paints, industrial chemicals, explosives, fertilizers, photographic material, and medical drugs. Belgium is the world's leading manufacturer of industrial

Opposite: **Glassmaking in Wallonia has been an industry in Belgium since the second century.**

A metal production plant in Belgium. Metal production in Belgium has declined over the last few decades.

carpets, playing cards, and billiard balls, and is known worldwide for its fine crystal glassware, coffee appliances, chocolate, and breweries. In fact, the world's largest brewing company to date is Belgian.

High-technology industries have grown in importance. These include industries such as biotechnology, lasers, microelectronics, office equipment, robotics, medical technology, aerospace, and telecommunications.

Whereas the old industries had depended on the canals and railway lines to move their goods, these new industries are more concerned with being close to highways. Most also prefer to be in Flanders, close to port facilities. Today Flanders is responsible for 60 percent of the nation's gross domestic product (GDP), compared with only 25 percent from Wallonia. The Flemish part of the country accounts for an even larger percentage of exports, producing some 70 percent of the total.

Although heavy industries, dependent on coal and iron, have traditionally been at the heart of the nation's wealth, these have declined over the last few decades and especially since the 1960s. This represents a prosperity shift from Wallonia where the ebbing traditional heavy industries are centered, to the more modernized Flanders. The textile industry has also been severely reduced due to competition from third world countries where wages are far lower.

The old industrial plants, notably around Liège and Charleroi, are still struggling to modernize, though several former industrial giants have survived by becoming smaller and more streamlined. Nonetheless, Wallonia's economy remains relatively depressed, and in 2005 the Wallonia government launched what it dubbed the region's Marshall Plan. Since the original Marshall Plan funded the reconstruction of Europe after World War II, this name alone gives an idea of the scale of the challenge. The plan consists of massive public investments (around $1.6 billion) to promote and develop training, research, business support, innovation, and enterprise.

In the 19th century Belgium was the first country on the European continent to join the industrial revolution, which had begun in Great Britain, resulting in the large-scale replacement of hand tools with machines.

POWER AND TRANSPORTATION

Belgium's industry was traditionally powered by its coal fields. Coal production reached its peak in 1953 when 33 million tons of coal were mined. By the 1980s that figure was down to 7 million. Gas, nuclear power,

RESEARCH

One reason Belgian industry has been so successful in adapting to new trends is that the country has made a big commitment to industrial research. There is talk in Belgium of a third industrial revolution, a collaboration between science and industry.

Research centers include Louvain University, which has undertaken extensive research into human gene technology, and the IMEC center, which works in microelectronics and microchip research. Ghent has the Plant Genetic Systems bacteria bank, and Liège is the home of an important space research center. Belgium is also leading the way in laser research.

So far, nine Belgians have won a Nobel Prize, five for science. The most recent winners are Ilya Prigogine, who won the prize for chemistry in 1977, and Albert Claude, who received the prize for medicine and physiology in 1974.

The first nuclear power plant at Doel near Antwerp was built along the Schelde River and came into operation in 1974.

and oil have since become far more important energy sources. One by one the coal mines were forced to close, causing considerable hardships in the coal-mining communities. The last Walloon coal mine closed in 1984. The Zolder and Beringen mines in Limburg continued operations for several more years but at last closed in 1992. This left the country completely dependent on imported fuel sources. Although Belgium does not have an oil production industry, Antwerp nonetheless has the biggest petrochemical refinery in Europe and Belgium reexports around 40 percent of its oil imports.

For years Belgium made a major commitment to nuclear power, and today nuclear energy meets 58 percent of the nation's energy needs. The national electricity generating company, Electrobel (recently bought by the French company Suez), operates seven nuclear power stations at two locations: Doel, close to Antwerp, which opened in 1974; and Tihange. Environmentalists, though, are concerned at the prospect of having so much nuclear activity in such a small country, and in 2002 the government announced plans to phase out nuclear power generation by 2025.

The plan is to focus instead on renewable energy sources, notably solar and wind power.

Because of the presence of good harbors and an excellent transportation network, Belgium has been described as the gateway to Europe. Antwerp ranks as the fifth busiest port in the world and the second busiest in Europe after Rotterdam; it is also regarded as one of the most efficient ports in the world. Considerable money has gone into expanding other harbors around the country. To transport goods to the port, Belgium has over 2,000 miles (3,218 km) of railway lines, most of which are electrified. There is also a very extensive road system, including 1,072 miles (1,725 km) of toll-free expressways. Nearly 1,000 miles (1,609 km) of waterways are in regular commercial use, and Liège remains one of Europe's busiest river ports. The Meuse and the Schelde rivers form the heart of this system, and they are linked by the 80 mile- (129 km-) long Albert Canal. The country's largest canal, it was completed in 1939 to connect Liège with Antwerp and can handle barges weighing up to 2,000 tons. Transportation along the smaller Canal du Centre between La Louvière and Thieu is now four hours faster than before since the installation of a unique hydraulic boat lift at Strépy-Thieu that raises barges by a vertical 240 feet (73 m). Other important canals link Ghent, Brussels, and Bruges with the sea. Approximately 60 percent of goods are transported by road, 20 percent by rail, and the rest by boat.

Belgium is too small to require regular domestic air links, but it is well connected with flights to other countries. Brussels (Zaventem) is the most important of Belgium's five international airports, and Belgium is the European hub for several international freight-forwarding corporations. Belgium's national airline, SABENA, was declared bankrupt in 2001 but there remain three locally based airlines, SN Brussels, Virgin Express, and VLM. SN Brussels offers many useful connections to African cities.

Fishing for shrimp along the North Sea coast is still done in the traditional way.

AGRICULTURE AND FISHING

Today farming employs less than 2 percent of the workforce, and most farms are family-owned enterprises. The amount of land being used for agriculture is decreasing, but Belgian farmers use extremely modern methods and are actually producing more than ever. Productivity is also raised by factors such as higher quality seeds and plants and better soil preparation. Belgian farmers provide one-fifth of the nation's food requirements.

The major crops are sugar beets, potatoes, and wheat, followed by barley, corn, and oats. Much of the grain goes to feed livestock. Annually, around 11 million pigs and 850,000 cows are butchered; over 700 million gallons (2.7 billion l) of milk are produced in the dairy industry, whose products form an important part of the Belgian diet. Different regions specialize in different products. The soil in northeastern Ardennes is used only for pasture, but horticulture is encouraged in Ghent. Where the soil is sandy, farmers tend to specialize in pig and chicken farming. Hops are grown, particularly around Poperinge. Fruit is harvested in southern Flanders.

Fishing is of relatively minor importance to the Belgian economy but adds character to the coastal ports of Ostend and Nieuwpoort. About 95 percent of the catch consists of fish, most valuably sole, with crustaceans and mollusks making up the rest. However, the famous "Belgian" mussels are actually produced at Yerseke just across the Dutch border. Small and supremely tasty, gray shrimps are collected mostly around Ostend and are a highly prized delicacy.

THE WORKFORCE

The population of Belgium is just over 10 million people. Statisticians classify those between the ages of 15 and 64 as the potentially active workforce, around 4.8 million, of which approximately 60 percent are employed. Some 7.6 percent of all active-aged Belgians are officially considered unemployed, but the figures are lower in Flanders, higher in Wallonia, and highest of all in Brussels-Capital Region (14.7 percent).

Today about 74 percent of the workforce is employed in service industries, such as education, transport, the hotel and hospitality business, banking, and finance. Belgium exports a growing number of services, with Belgian consultants and financial advisers working around the world. Belgians are productive workers who take pride

Most of Belgium's working women are employed by the service sector and in light industries, such as food and textile production.

in a job well done. The Belgian workforce is well trained and is often multilingual, which is the main reason so many foreign companies have invested in the country. Indeed, many secretarial and white-collar jobs expect candidates to speak a minimum of two or three languages fluently. In general, union membership is strong, union-employer consultative councils are often compulsory, and firing union representatives can prove very costly to an employer.

The Belgian government consults closely with workers, and wages and working conditions compare favorably with those in most other countries. The average workweek is 38 hours, and Belgians typically have four weeks' worth of vacation a year.

ENVIRONMENT

BELGIANS IN GENERAL are relatively environmentally conscious. Ecological parties formed part of the ruling government coalition between 1999 and 2003. Many Belgians are happy about recent eco taxes that encourage people to think about the environment when shopping and making other lifestyle decisions.

GREENHOUSE GASES AND CARBON EMISSIONS

Recent severe changes in the environment have been bringing unpredictable weather—colder winters and hotter summers. Most scientists consider this climate change to be due to global warming, caused by the emission of greenhouse gases, notably carbon dioxide, which are produced when fossil fuels such as natural gas, gasoline, and other petroleum products are combusted. Like most developed nations, Belgium has ratified the Kyoto Protocol, which is designed to slow down greenhouse gas production. This means that Belgium has pledged to reduce its emissions by 7.5 percent by 2012. To work toward this goal, the government is confronting the problem on both large (macro) and personal levels.

On the personal level, public education programs are conducted to show, for example, how to save money as well as reduce energy consumption by regularly defrosting refrigerators, using high-performance lamps, or washing clothes on low-temperature cycles. Washing machines are taxed according to their energy-efficiency grading, prompting individuals to choose power-efficient appliances. Each of Belgium's three regions has a series of grants available for encouraging fuel-efficiency measures in

Above: **Windmills can reduce the occurence of global warming.**

Opposite: **A nuclear power plant along Port Antwerp.**

43

Cooling towers of the nuclear power plant of Tihange, Namur, Belgium.

the home such as installing loft insulation (usually fiberglass matting in rolls), double glazing windows, and converting heating systems to high-efficiency condensation-type gas boilers. Despite relatively low sunshine figures, tax and grant incentives mean that home owners are starting to find it profitable to install solar roof panels.

On a macro level, considerable investments have been made in wind turbines, though some local people dislike the giant windmills as they feel these spoil their scenery. Belgium's electricity-generating system is now highly dependent on nuclear power. Although these produce no greenhouse gases and are thus considered useful in decelerating global warming, they are potentially very dangerous if an accident should occur. Furthermore, nuclear waste is extremely toxic and difficult to dispose of. In 2002, under pressure from environmentalist parties, the government agreed to scrap all nuclear power stations by 2025. This further pushes the need to develop renewable and sustainable energy sources.

GARBAGE, RECYCLING, AND REUSE

Garbage collection systems vary greatly within Belgium as each town or municipality organizes its own. Nonetheless, it is common for most towns to encourage a division of waste into various classes to allow for easy and efficient recycling. There might be special collection days for paper, plastics and metals, garden and other organic waste, and general refuse.

Householders typically pay for waste collection by the number of bags, but the charge for the collection of recyclable waste is cheaper per bag than for general garbage. This encourages people to think green.

Each region (Flanders, Wallonia, and Brussels) has its own recycling agency. These are also charged with educating the public to better understand the waste management systems.

Glassware is rarely included in household garbage collections. Instead people are encouraged to use bottle-bank collection points for jars and wine bottles. Many other bottles, especially beer bottles, have a paid deposit, so the consumer is financially rewarded to take those bottles back to the seller for washing and reuse. Most Belgian families buy beer in 24-bottle crates, and this deposit costs almost as much as the beer. When the contents are finished, one returns the bottles to the supermarket, feeding the crate and bottles into a special bottle-counting machine that registers the value of the bottles and returns the deposit as an electronic voucher. This can be used like cash at the checkout.

Waste segregation is encouraged in Belgium for efficient collection and recycling.

ECO TAXES

Since 1993, eco taxes have been applied to encourage recycling and inculcate an environment-friendly mentality among citizens and businesses.

Batteries are a common source of hazardous waste in family garbage. Belgium's high profile campaign to recycle batteries has been aided by eco taxes and also by a major awareness campaign. As a result, almost every family keeps old batteries out of their trash, using the special envelopes provided by BEBAT, the battery recycling organization, instead.

Since 2001 a recycling contribution eco tax has been added to the price of most electronic equipment. The tax has been cleverly calculated

A collection bin for environment-friendly separation of trash for recycling.

so that the tax charged will rise with the degree of difficulty with which a product can be recycled. This encourages manufacturers to think about the environment when designing their devices and packaging. Businesses selling electronics now must also think about their products' disposability. That is because "take-back" legislation provides that any customer buying a qualifying product can take to the store the old version that he or she is replacing. The system is gradually growing in scope.

As in most European countries, the tax on gasoline is extremely high, which is why a gallon of gas costs around $6, or Euro 1.35 per liter. The idea of these high prices is to encourage people to use public transportation and thus reduce both traffic congestion and the emission level of greenhouse gases that cause global warming.

In Belgium, however, this approach is not especially successful because the public transportation system is not usually convenient enough. There is another series of taxes on cars, charged according to their fuel efficiency: if a car has low carbon dioxide emissions and high fuel efficiency, the owner will pay much lower rates.

WATER

Belgium is home to several major commercial mineral springs and the world's original spa at, yes, Spa. If one goes to a restaurant in Belgium and asks for a glass of water, one will always get bottled or mineral water. Waiters will be shocked if tap water is requested instead and might refuse to serve it. This is purely convention and clever economics. In fact Belgian tap water is perfectly good to drink and is subjected to around 50 different tests and checks to ensure that it is safe for consumption.

Yet even at home many Belgians drink bottled water. In 2004 a tax was added to plastic bottles in an attempt to fund their recycling and discourage the use of disposable bottles. However, this caused annoyance among Belgium's powerful water bottlers. The tax was removed in mid-2005.

THE NORTH SEA

Belgium has 41 miles (66.5 km) of coastline facing the North Sea—a sensitive ecosystem under a great deal of pressure from intense human activities, and surrounded on three sides by densely populated, industrialized countries. Rivers flowing into the sea carry effluent and sometimes toxic industrial discharges. Some ecologists suggest that such pollution might have contributed to the viral diseases that decimated the North Sea seal populations in the 1980s and that struck again in 2002.

Considerable quantities of oil and gas are extracted from deep beneath the North Sea, while its waters are crisscrossed by some of the world's busiest shipping routes. Both these activities add to the threat of water pollution, whether from small oil spills or catastrophic accidents involving tankers or oil rigs.

Historically, fishing has been a major industry in the North Sea and around 5 percent of the world's total fish catch is still caught here. To preserve fish stocks, stringent EU quotas on catches have been imposed over recent decades. This has partly reversed the devastating effects of previous overfishing. However, many fish-species populations have not rebounded as quickly as had been predicted. Scientists suspect that this might be linked to a slow rise in sea temperatures due to global warming. Cold-water fish such as cod are increasingly found farther north in subarctic waters, and some predict that they will become extinct in the North Sea over time. Meanwhile, warmer water fish, such as the mullet, squid, and lobster, are becoming more common.

Belgium's short coastline culminates at Het Zwin, a stretch of protected salt marshes that attract thousands of waterbirds, including migrating swans and reed geese. Eagle owls can also be spotted here. Farther south are some beautiful dunes and many miles of wide, sandy beaches. Despite the unpredictable weather, beaches are backed by heavily developed tourist resorts aimed mainly at the domestic market of weekend visitors, accounting for about 30 million visits per year. This economically important recreation and hospitality industry is directly impacted by environmental concerns over the quality of the North Sea water. At times the sea is even considered unsafe for swimming. However, the Flemish Environment Agency now marks the beaches to alert swimmers to the water quality. Smiley, sad, or neutral face symbols are posted according to the results of seawater tests. Samplings are carried out at least twice weekly in summer. Meanwhile, a department of the Royal Belgian Institute of Natural Sciences (RBINS) studies the ecosystems of the North Sea, using mathematical modeling techniques to assess the condition of the marine environment.

Waterbirds are often spotted along the North Sea coastline.

BELGIANS

BELGIUM'S POPULATION OF JUST over 10 million consists of two major communities: the Flemish speaking and the French speaking (Francophone). There is also a smaller community of German speakers, and German is Belgium's third official language.

TWO DIFFERENT PEOPLES

The Flemings and the Walloons make up the vast majority of Belgians. The Flemings mostly live in the north and speak Flemish, a version of Dutch. Most Belgians speak a version of French and are termed Francophones. They live mostly in Brussels and Wallonia. The term Walloon is often used to describe people from Wallonia, but to most Belgians it refers more specifically to speakers of various thick and often hardly intelligible dialects of French. Walloons trace their ancestry back to the Celtic Belgae tribes who were reputed to be ferocious fighters. After the Belgae were conquered by Rome about 52 B.C., they started to integrate with their Roman invaders, so their language became Latinized.

Centuries of intermingling means that there is no immediately apparent racial or physical difference between Flemings and Walloons, although people from Wallonia tend to be marginally shorter than those from Flanders. In the last century considerable immigration into Wallonia has further added to the Mediterranean looks of some Walloons, while typical natives of Flanders are somewhat more likely to be blond and blue-eyed in the Viking-Germanic mold.

In reality, the deep divisions in Belgian society are almost entirely a matter of language and culture.

Above: **Belgian children at play.**

Opposite: **A Belgian couple wearing traditional costumes for a Belgian festival at the Grand Place in Brussels.**

Belgian men donning identical red scarves for a festival. Belgians make a point of being friendly and enjoying the good life.

Belgians are less concerned about the destiny of nations than of their own region. A Belgian is more attached to the city that gives character to his or her region and countryside.

For centuries French was the legal and court language, and historically Francophones did not think well of their Flemish-speaking neighbors. Flemish elites in cities like Antwerp and Ghent would often associate the French language with prestige. By the 19th century Wallonia, the home of most mining and heavy industry, was vastly more economically powerful than Flanders.

Flemish people who did not speak French were unable to understand legal procedures. In several infamous cases during World War I, soldiers were court-martialed and executed for failing to carry out orders that they simply did not understand because they did not speak French. Understandably, this caused a great sense of injustice and a newly vibrant Flemish literature scene pushed heavily for linguistic equality.

During the 20th century this was not only achieved but the whole economic balance of the country shifted. Flanders, once the poor half of Belgium, is now considerably wealthier than Wallonia. Increasingly, more Flemish people have started to feel that their enterprise is wasted by having to help support the economically ailing south. Others, however, realize that as a rich part of the EU, an independent Flanders could end up subsidizing poorer nations from Poland to Portugal, so they consider it better to subsidize Wallonia, which is closer to home and familiar.

THE GERMANS—BELGIUM'S THIRD GROUP

German was recognized as one of Belgium's official languages in 1963. However there are only around 70,000 German-speaking Belgians. They live in the Ostkantonen, a small strip of land around the town of Eupen, close to the German border. This region was given to Belgium by the Treaty of Versailles after World War I to help make amends for the war. The area was briefly annexed by Germany during World War II but was returned to Belgium after the Allied armies liberated the country in 1944.

Residents of German-speaking Belgium in front of a German information center.

Most people from this region describe themselves as Belgians who happen to speak German. Most are bilingual, in French as the children start learning French in the first grade and then another language as they grow older. People in this region still feel proud about their German culture and language.

The German minority have benefited from the ongoing struggle between Belgium's two larger language groups, and they have acquired considerable independence without ever really campaigning for it. There are a German radio station and television service for the area and a few small German newspapers. Economically, the area has strong links with Germany. The large German city of Aachen is just across the border, and many people commute there to work and shop.

LES MAROLLES—A WORLD OF ITS OWN

Les Marolles (LEH mah-ROHL) is the old working-class region of Brussels and consists of the alleyways that lie in the shadow of the gigantic Court of Justice. Traditionally, the people living there were employed as low-paid manual workers or were involved in small-scale trading.

Like the London Cockneys, the people here developed their own Marollien (mah-roh-LYEAN) dialect and have a special sense of humor. The Marolles dialect, a version of French with many Flemish words mixed in, was the result of workers from both language groups living closely together in these narrow streets. The dialect even retained some words from Spanish, a legacy from the days when the soldiers of Philip II roamed the crowded streets.

In recent decades greater mobility, city regeneration, and a considerable influx of immigrants to the Marolles means that the unique spirit and culture of the area has virtually died out. Still, some local street signs remain trilingual (Flemish, French, and Marollien) and in certain cafés one will find locals speaking a diluted form of Marollien dialect. The best place to look and to immerse oneself in the region's culture is around the Vossenplein or Place de Jeu de Balle where there is a flea market early each morning.

HOW THE BELGIANS SEE THEMSELVES

Sometimes it is hard to see what keeps Belgium's linguistically divided peoples together. But in fact there are several common characteristics that cross the Francophone-Flemish barrier. Both communities are overwhelmingly, if only nominally, Roman Catholic, sharing a curious mixture of conservative mind-set with outwardly liberal attitudes. Both communities might dislike one another, but both prefer each other to their other near neighbors: Francophone Belgians find French people typically arrogant while the Flemish tend to see their Dutch neighbors as humorless and tightfisted. On either side of the linguistic divide, Belgians delight in a quietly indulgent good life, with fine food and plenty of it washed down with some of the world's best beers. Both communities show an entertainingly deadpan style of conversation where the borderline between grumbling and humor is often hard to spot.

By necessity, living in such a fragmented society has made Belgians particularly adept at compromising, making Belgium a kind of Europe in miniature. Living in a small country, many Belgians have a remarkably open-minded view of the world. Most Belgians consider themselves to be reasonably easygoing but at the same time independent and capable of being quite stubborn when the need arises.

Belgians taking a sunny break in the park.

By the high standards expected in Western Europe, Belgium has traditionally been seen as a place where mild corruption and nepotism (favoritism) were the norm. There have been some improvements in recent years, and today Belgium stands at the 19th position, together with Ireland, in the 2005 Transparency International's Corruption Perceptions Index. Nonetheless, having the right connections remains very useful and is still very much part of the Belgian way of life. Giving corporate gifts and inducements is rarely seen to be corrupt, but merely oiling the wheels of personal interactions.

FOREIGNERS

Belgium's healthy economy, its many multinational organizations, and its pan-European institutions attract many people from other countries. As of 2003, 8.2 percent of the officially registered population were foreigners. The majority of foreigners are from other EU countries, especially France and the Netherlands. However, when Belgians use the term "foreigners," they are usually referring to immigrants, especially of Turkish or North African origin.

In the 1960s immigration was encouraged by the government as Belgium had a shortage of labor. The first waves of immigrants came mainly from Italy and, later, Morocco and Turkey. Many became Belgian citizens and a part of the nation's increasingly mixed community. Others integrated into Belgian society but chose to keep their original nationality. At first some did this to avoid doing national service in the Belgian armed forces, though such service is no longer required. People from the former African colonies add another dimension to the ethnic mixture, though their numbers are comparatively small.

Belgian laws protect the ethnic and religious freedoms of all people, but social and cultural problems remain. Some immigrants have found it difficult to integrate with the rest of the population, and there is a tendency

Belgium's ethnic and cultural diversity is evident in the schools of Brussels and other regions with a high concentration of immigrants.

A NEW GENERATION OF IMMIGRANTS

A new generation of children of immigrants is achieving fame in Belgian society. Wallonia's minister-president, Elio Di Ruppo (*right*) is the first Italian Belgian to make any real impact on politics. He is also mayor of Mons and leader of the PS Francophone Socialist party. Other Italian-Belgian celebrities include top-selling singer Salvator Adamo and soccer star turned restaurateur Enzo Scifo. Algerian-born Faouzia Hariche is one of the best known Brussels city politicians. Surinam-born Alida Neslo was one of the first black hosts on Flemish television. African Belgian Mbo Mpenza is currently the star striker of the Red Devils, Belgium's national soccer team.

to group together in certain areas. About 12 percent of the people legally living in Brussels are of non-European origin, though there are thought to be almost as many living without legitimate papers. Most Italian Belgians are concentrated around Charleroi and the areas of heavy industry in Wallonia and the mining towns in Limburg (northeast Belgium). Towns like Waterloo on Brussels's southern outskirts have attracted many nationalities of mostly wealthy white-collar expatriates, and have international and Scandinavian schools. Almost every Belgian town has at least a few families of Kurds, Turks, and Chinese generally involved in the catering trade or operating small shops, which are usually well appreciated as they tend to stay open for longer hours than those owned by Belgians. Increasing numbers of Eastern Europeans also live in Belgium, often working illegally as domestic helpers and casual day laborers.

Many ordinary Belgian citizens see immigration as one of the most important issues that affect the future of their country. There is a common perception that "foreigners," are responsible for a variety of socioeconomic problems and petty crime. Such sentiments are most extreme in Flanders, even though that region has the lowest percentage of resident foreigners or immigrants. The extremist Vlaams Belang party has taken advantage of this. Their predecessor party, Vlaams Blok, campaigned under the slogan "Our Own People First" until it was outlawed as racist. Much to Belgium's embarrassment, Vlaams Belang has become one of the biggest parties in Flanders.

Citizens of Belgium from non-Belgian EU nations can vote in municipal and national elections.

LIFESTYLE

BELGIANS TRADITIONALLY WITHDRAW into small, familiar groups. They feel the most comfortable in their own homes and their own communities. They place great importance on family, friends, and food.

HOUSING

There is a popular expression that goes like this: "Every Belgian is born with a brick in the stomach." This reflects the dream that many Belgians have to design and build their own homes. Traditionally, old Flemish houses had attractive Dutch-style stepped side gables that created distinctively photogenic town centers. These days, however, despite Belgium's rich architectural heritage and the people's passion for designing their own homes, popular building styles are surprisingly dour and functional. Houses typically are made of brick with tiled roofing, often finished with a coat of whitewashed plaster. In suburban areas luxurious "villas" (single-family houses) are relatively common, along with cheaper duplex units and apartment buildings. In cities, apartments and connected townhouses are more common.

Particularly high taxes imposed on the purchase and sale of houses means that once Belgians have bought or built a home, they are unlikely to move again. Therefore, choosing where to buy or build is very important. Generally, the most popular areas to live in are in the outer suburbs or the villages just beyond city limits. This has resulted in many Belgians commuting considerable distances to work, causing extensive rush-hour traffic congestion. The trend of building in the increasingly crowded

Above: **Houses of all styles, modern and classic, mingle throughout the Belgian landscape.**

Opposite: **Belgians love to spend time with their families or friends.**

countryside has also caused more and more houses to appear along once-rural roads, undermining the very appeal of these areas. Differences between rural and urban lifestyles are also diminishing, although regional differences and identities remain pronounced.

JOBS, CARS, AND CLOTHES

As in most successful capitalist nations, there is considerable social pressure to find good jobs, establish strong careers, and gain promotions. However, most Belgians feel that one works to live rather than lives to work. So although Belgians work hard to get ahead, they will not necessarily be keen on advancement if it requires giving up their holidays or weekends.

Many of the expensive cars that seem so common on Belgium's roads are provided by companies to their employees as a tax-efficient perk.

Advertising encourages the pursuit of name-branded material possessions. However, showy displays of wealth and status are frowned upon. To impress others, one's choice of status symbols should be carefully targeted and not ostentatious. Foreign visitors often notice the remarkable number of expensive automobiles and jump to the conclusion that Belgians are extravagant with their cars. In reality, a very high percentage of these fine vehicles are company cars. Employees who drive them could rarely ever afford to buy such expensive models. Both businesses and employees find that a leased company car is a handy way for everyone to avoid paying taxes on new cars.

Many people acknowledge that Belgians are not particularly safe drivers. Despite strict laws to make roads safer, there are often bad

accidents. Unless the police are in sight, many drivers tend to ignore the minor regulations. Cars weave through traffic at high speeds, even in places where that means rattling over old cobblestoned streets.

Non-European drivers should be aware of the terrifying "right-priority" rule. This gives priority at any unmarked junction to the vehicle that arrives from the right, even when there is a very small lane leading onto a major through road. The country also has to grapple with the hazards of drunk and reckless driving. It is not surprising, given these problems, along with some very poor road signs, ambiguous pedestrian priorities, and hard-to-understand expressway junctions, that Belgium has the second worst per-capita road fatality rate in Western Europe (after Portugal).

If Belgians put less emphasis on clothing than the French or Italians, they still like to look good. Particularly in Brussels, it is evident that people invest a great deal of care and money in their appearance. The clothing budget of most Belgians is spent on good quality apparel. The dress code is quite formal. In offices, men are still expected to wear jackets, although in winter, as a concession to the cold, a jacket might be replaced by a smart wool sweater. It is quite acceptable for women to wear pants to work.

Annually Belgium suffers 45,000–50,000 road accidents, causing around 1,350 deaths. Despite educational campaigns, fast cars and a laissez-faire attitude toward driving after drinking alcohol are most often to blame. Belgium's roads have very poor road signs and hard-to-understand expressway junctions, most notoriously the Carrefour Leonard (Leonard Crossing) on the ring road around Brussels.

Having a chat or just watching people go by while sitting on a bench in a village.

SOCIAL INTERACTIONS

Belgians are not shy, but they are typically quite reserved. It would be considered unusual for a stranger to try to strike up a conversation in public. In stores it is normal good manners to say "good day" to a shopkeeper or checkout clerk before proceeding with a purchase. However, it is uncommon to ask "How are you doing?" to those you do not already know. When introduced to strangers, Belgians are generally formal and polite, but do not expect effusive interest. Generally Belgian friendships must be won over a considerable period, and breaking into a social group takes some effort and commitment. Friendly neighbors nod greetings to one another or stop to chat outside their homes, but they wouldn't necessarily expect to be invited inside even after several years of acquaintance. Although people vary greatly, it is unusual to drop in on a Belgian friend without telephoning ahead. When visiting, it is typical to bring flowers, wine, or a small gift, depending on the occasion.

Between strangers, a handshake is usually appropriate. The two parties introducing themselves simply utter their names. Colleagues greeting each other at the start of another day at work might also shake hands in a relaxed way. Close friends and family are more likely to kiss one another. The full Belgian kiss greeting is three times on alternating cheeks. The procedure is often shortened to a single cheek peck especially when there are many people to greet. Indeed, in Flanders some people consider a single kiss to be more generally appropriate, though rules are not hard and fast. Men are less likely to kiss one another than women, but male relations and close friends may do so.

When answering the telephone, most Belgians simply announce their name or say "Hallo?"

A family outing on a sunny day along a coastal promenade.

FAMILY AND CHILDREN

Due to a low birth rate (10.48 per 1,000) and an even lower death rate (10.2 per 1,000), Belgium's population is aging. However, with over 10.3 million inhabitants—over 875 per square mile (337 per square km)—Belgium is still the second-most-densely populated country in Europe.

The average family size at the start of the 20th century was five people. This number declined until after World War II. During the postwar baby boom the average family had three children. This number has now dropped to almost two children throughout the country, even in the Flemish region, which traditionally had a higher birth rate than the rest of the nation. One factor is that more men and women choose to stay single or to delay marriage and having children. Divorce has risen dramatically over the recent decades.

LOOKED AFTER BY THE STATE

Belgium has a highly developed system of social services and spends more on social protection than the European average. The system costs the government almost 35% of the GDP. Belgians receive a family allowance, free education and scholarships for advanced education, health care, pensions, and welfare benefits for the unemployed.

Health care alone accounts for 7 percent of the gross national budget, and a large proportion of the total is expended on the health of senior citizens. A low birth rate and an excellent health-care system have brought a noticeable change in the average age of the population. At the start of the 20th century, one out of every 15 Belgians was over 60. Today the figure is one out of every five. Belgian men can expect to live to an average age of 72, women to 79. The most common causes of death are cancer and heart disease.

The aging of the population has created some serious social and economic problems. The country faces a rising bill for nursing and pensions. In addition, higher unemployment, a lower birth rate, and more single-parent families make the Belgian social protection system weigh heavily on the state budget. A restructuring to moderate costs was begun in 1981. A portion of the health-care costs are now chargeable to patients. Welfare payments to the longtime unemployed are being gradually lowered.

Belgian children are expected to work hard in school and are generally thought of as being well disciplined. Yet shocking statistics revealed in 2005 that 40 percent of Belgian children have tried marijuana by the age of 18. At the same time, Belgian children have become increasingly status conscious; great importance is attached to having the latest electronic toys and fashionable clothes. Children's birthdays are usually occasions for a small party with friends, games, and presents. After the 18th birthday people attach less significance to the event, but birthdays are still times for the family to get together and celebrate.

Family and children

Although church attendance is low, most Roman Catholic children still attach great importance to the ceremony of their first Holy Communion at age 12. For several weeks beforehand, all the children taking Holy Communion receive religious instruction, then on the big day they parade through the streets to the church. Traditionally boys and girls alike wore white clothing for this occasion, though these days boys tend to simply wear their Sunday-best clothes. The event is seen as an important stage in growing up, and the children receive presents from their relatives. In many ways it has become more of a big family party than a religious occasion.

Unlike the United States, there is no real tradition for Belgian children to have part-time or weekend jobs. In large part this is due to the tax system that until 2005 allowed children only 23 days of paid work per year (in summer vacations only), after which full social security payments become due and their families could lose fiscal or family-support benefits. At 18, Belgians can vote, drive, and leave school.

Young adults tend to live with their parents until they can afford their own home or marry. They seem to have good relationships, and they have respect for their parents. But where 50 years ago many Belgian families lived in large houses with several generations staying together, young families today prefer to have their own homes, as they do all over the Western world.

As a result, senior housing is becoming more common in both the cities and suburbs. In fact, there is a feeling that Belgian society is a little too quick to send older people to such homes. In the villages more emphasis is put on building small apartments or cottages for older people. There it is easier for them to enjoy their privacy and to maintain friendships, in addition to having the advantages of village services such as health care and home delivery of groceries

In January 2003 Belgium became the second country to recognize marriage between same-sex couples. This allows for equality of tax breaks and automatic inheritance rights. Child adoption rights for gay couples was approved by the House of Representatives in December 2005.

Children file past the
graffiti-covered wall of
their school.

EDUCATION

Flemish-, French-, and German-speaking communities each has its own separate education ministry, and education is given in the regional language. Education is compulsory until the age of 18, and one out of every four students continues their education beyond this point. Schools in Belgium are run both by the government and by private organizations, notably the Catholic church. Generally Catholic schools have the best reputation for educational standards. Funds for both state and private schools are provided by the government, so education is essentially free, except in international schools, which are very expensive but mostly cater to expatriate families. Nonetheless, parents must still fund school trips and pay a small charge for photocopies, library fees, composition books, and a school-rules manual. Parents are also expected to buy all schoolbooks, and many children will get some money back by selling these at the end of the year. The curriculum for both primary and secondary education is guided by education inspectors.

Belgian children usually start kindergarten at the age of three, but many working parents enroll their toddlers in preschool even before that age. At age six children proceed to primary school, which lasts for six years. When they are 12 years old, they move into secondary school, which involves a great deal more of research-based study and a choice of difficult subject options. Normally only those who complete the sixth grade of secondary school education are eligible for university, though it is technically possible for vocational school students to qualify by completing an extra (seventh) year of school.

Students who fail exams have to repeat the year's curriculum. Those who do not do well in academic schools are encouraged to seek work apprenticeships or entry to a vocational school, which develops practical skills.

Belgium has a 500-year history of university education, with the Catholic University of Leuven being a notable international center of learning and research. Today a network of 19 universities and other institutions of higher learning educate some 100,000 students a year. Students have to complete two cycles—one of general studies and one of specialized studies— that last two to three years each before being awarded a degree that leads to a professional life. Generally only around 40 percent succeed in passing the first year. During the last few decades increased close cooperation with Belgian industries has helped various universities join world leaders in scientific research and training.

The school year starts on September 1 each year, unless it falls on a weekend. This is called the rentrée. *It is a focus for the media, and supermarkets fill with school materials and thousands of new "cartables" (student backpacks). Suddenly the roads, which were pleasantly empty all summer, are congested again at rush hour.*

ROLE OF WOMEN

The last few decades have seen a remarkable feminization of the workforce in Belgium: in 1970 only 32 percent of active-aged women worked. This has now risen to over 51 percent. Laws passed in 1978 guarantee men and women equal legal and social opportunities, and equal wages for equal work. Of those officially classified as unemployed, there is no longer a substantial difference between men (6.7 percent) and women (8.7 percent). Claims of

Most working women in Belgium still have to combine their professional life with the usual tasks at home.

sexual harassment, or women receiving unfair treatment at work, are taken seriously, although there is often a marked difference between what Belgians and Americans consider as sexist.

A high percentage of working women are employed in the services and the government sector, and others work in industry and agriculture. Although there has yet to be a female prime minister, six of the 21 ministers and state secretaries in the national government are women. Highly educated women hold key positions in judiciary and diplomatic fields, and the government campaigns to encourage women to aim for positions as decision makers and managers in industry, the media, and the business world.

Government policy encourages working women to combine professional and family life: child care helps women return to work quickly if they wish, but it is also possible for mothers to take up to four months leave to care for their new babies. Especially among older working couples, however, it is still relatively unusual for a man to stay home to look after young children. In general, working women still spend more time doing domestic chores than their male working partners: 36 and 22 hours respectively per week.

THE FUTURE

Despite the high level of autonomy given to the federation, linguistic differences and tensions remain overwhelmingly Belgium's most sensitive issue. Many locals doubt whether the country will survive as a single unit for their lifetimes—or even for the next decade.

Unemployment and national debt remain major concerns for many Belgians. Those who have lost their jobs in the old industrial areas and lack any other qualifications are facing up to the fact that they might be out of work for years. Young people attending university are also worried about finding work. As people age, they are becoming increasingly nervous about their pensions: controversial plans to prevent early retirement at the age of 58 and to change many pension benefits caused a one-day national strike in 2005, the first in 12 years.

Immigration is another issue that disturbs many people; there is a widely held view that too many foreigners are coming to live in Belgium. This is reflected in recent election results that gave considerable support to right-wing parties promising to control immigration.

Taxes are the fourth great concern. Nobody likes taxes, but in Belgium, tax dodging is seen as something of a national sport. Since many people try to avoid taxes, the government is moving to generally reduce taxation, hoping that in the end more people will pay so that the books will still balance. A less-than-successful "tax amnesty" in 2004 tried to persuade Belgians to bring home their secret savings from foreign bank accounts, notably in low-tax Luxembourg.

Crime is less of a worry than in the United States and in other parts of Europe. One reason is that the possession of weapons is strictly controlled. But there is a rising concern over crime. The many expensive cars and the relative ease of escaping across unsecured national borders into neighboring countries have encouraged an increased frequency of carjacking. Figures of the year 2005 showed that burglaries were running at over 30,000 per year, making it statistically probable that a family would be burgled at least once during their lifetime. Although statistics have yet to prove it conclusively, it is commonly believed that organized criminal gangs from Eastern Europe are behind many of the incidents. Social problems of graffiti and assault on public transportation employees are also increasing.

RELIGION

AT THE START OF THE FIFTH century, the warlike Franks moved into Belgium and overran most of the Roman settlements there. One of the Frankish leaders, King Clovis, converted to Christianity in the year 496. A diocese was established at Tongeren, and churches were built around the country as the new religion spread.

The seventh century saw Christianity spread more rapidly, especially during the reign of the Frankish king Charlemagne. Over the centuries Benedictine monasteries and abbeys became great cultural centers and major landowners, the clergy being allied with the local nobility. The 11th century has been called the Age of Faith, when people in both Flanders and Wallonia, and indeed in most of Europe, held unquestioning belief in Christianity.

Over the following centuries, however, Christianity became removed from the teachings of Christ. Priests increasingly "sold" salvation as a product, and the religion became more a form of social control than a source of spiritual inspiration. But things started to change with the development of printing. Educated people who could buy their own copies of the Bible, and read for themselves, discovered that many church practices had nothing to do with what the Bible said. The result was the rise of Protestantism, especially following Martin Luther's 1517 thesis. Luther was German, but the people of the Netherlands and Flanders, being among the wealthiest and best-educated people in Europe, were quick to follow. There was widespread burning of icons, attacks on Roman Catholic churches and, ultimately, the Dutch revolt against their Spanish rulers. Years of war followed, after which Holland became independent. But Belgium was retaken by ferociously pro-Catholic Spain, and the Belgian people were virtually forced to submit to strict, orthodox Catholicism.

Above: **The Roman Catholic church enjoyed a religious monopoly for centuries in Belgium, but later had to compete, sometimes bitterly, with other faiths, such as Protestantism.**

Opposite: **The Notre Dame Cathedral in Tournai, Belgium.**

Grand Romanesque and Gothic churches were built for hundreds of worshippers. Today these spacious buildings are completely filled only on special occasions.

EMPTY CHURCHES

Belgium is predominantly a Roman Catholic nation and the last country in northern Europe to have a Catholic monarch. Most national holidays are based on the Christian calendar, notably Christmas, Assumption, and Easter. Most of Belgium's greatest festivals, particularly their fabulous carnivals, are related to religion, albeit distantly.

Despite the common use of the term Catholic as a social label, few people regularly attend church. Attendance is slightly higher in Flanders than in Wallonia, and higher in villages than in urban communities. The church plays a role at funerals, and a priest typically visits bereaved families of the dead. Cemeteries themselves are generally plots of civic land not linked to a religious establishment. Although many Belgian couples enjoy holding a wedding ceremony in an old church, the legal act of marriage must always be conducted in the local town hall.

Despite the small congregations, Belgian churches still demonstrate a remarkable vitality, helped by the fact that the Belgian government pays the priests' wages. Congregations are involved in a whole range of community activities, and the buildings are well tended as well as decorated inside with candles and flowers. Churches also sponsor considerable missionary work and aid projects around the world.

RELIGIOUS ORDERS

Monasteries, convents, and abbeys, where people can remove themselves from the material world and devote their lives to God, are a small but important part of Belgian religious life. Although some of the abbeys and monasteries have closed, there are still people who seek life in a religious order.

From the middle of the 11th century onward, religious orders owned some of the richest farmland in Belgium. They became profitable commercial concerns. They used their wealth to help the poor and were important patrons of the arts. Many of the monks were themselves magnificent artists who have left wonderful treasures in the form of manuscripts, metalwork, statues, and paintings.

In convents and abbeys, nuns live in total seclusion and avoid any contact with the outside world.

Many different monastic orders are represented in Belgium, but it is the Cistercians who have probably had the greatest impact. In 1098 Robert of Molesme felt that the Benedictines had become too lax. So he left with a few followers to found the Cistercian order (at Cîteaux in France). By the end of the 12th century, the Cistercians had over 500 monasteries. The order emphasized the importance of manual work and had a great impact on farming techniques throughout the country. Trappists, the strictest of all Cistercians, even made a rule to maintain silence except when absolutely necessary.

Many monasteries today are best known for their brewing of beers and making of cheese. Brewing was originally important for health reasons, as

water supplies were often unsafe to drink. Later beer was sold to fund the
restoration and upkeep of the institutions, especially after the destruction
caused by the French invasion after the French Revolution. Belgium's most
famous beers are still produced by the Trappist abbeys of Orval, Rochefort,
Chimay, Westemalle, Westvleteren, and Achel.

The *Begijnhofven* (buh-GEYEN-hoVEN, *Beguinages* in French) were
special religious homes where women could enjoy fellow female company
and security within a religious atmosphere without taking vows. Mostly
confined to the Netherlands and Flanders, the movement is believed to
have been started by Lambert le Begue to help women who had lost
husbands and sons in the Crusades. The *Begijnhof* communities consisted
of a church, infirmary, weaving center, and small, individual houses around
a safely enclosed courtyard. The beautiful *Begijnhofven* of Flanders are
now recognized collectively by UNESCO as world heritage sites. There are
wonderful examples of the *Begijnhofven* in Bruges, Lier, Diest, Tongeren,
Leuven, and Turnhout.

PRIESTS

The Belgian Roman Catholic Church is led by the archbishop of Brussels
and Mechelen. Priests conduct the services and give the sermons.
They administer the sacraments, including baptism, hear confessions,
and provide spiritual direction to their community. Priests can be seen
at local events and helping with youth organizations.

Roman Catholic priests are not permitted to marry and women are not
allowed to become priests, a restriction that causes a serious shortage
of priests in Belgium. Because of this, rural priests are often expected to
look after several villages, making it impossible for them to have the same
personal contact with their congregations as their predecessors did a few

THE SAINTS

Although Belgium's different communities share the same religious heroes, Christian names usually have different forms in Flanders and Wallonia. That means that church names also appear different in each region.

The key figure in the Christian religion is Jesus (Jezus, in Flemish), whom believers considered to be the son of God, though his human mother, Mary (Maria, Marie), is also given considerable reverence by Catholics. Churches in her honor are usually named Our Lady (Onze Lieve Vrouw, Notre Dame). Others include Saint Peter (Petrus, Pièrre); the first pope, Saint Paul, the man who redesigned Christianity to appeal to a non-Jewish audience; dragon-fighting Saint George (Joris, Georges); and animal-loving Saint Francis (Frans, Francois) who is known as Tchantchès in Walloon and humorously as Suske in Marrolien.

Several saints played important roles in the early days of Christianity in Belgium, and some of the early saints, such as Saint Amandus and his pupil Saint Bavo, came from noble families.

Saint Servatius was a priest from Armenia who became the first bishop of the Netherlands. Although usually associated with Maastricht, he was also based at the Belgian city of Tongeren and prophesied the invasion of Gaul by the Huns. Foreseeing the violent times ahead, he went on a pilgrimage to pray for the safety of his flock and died of fever on his return to Belgium in A.D. 384.

Saint Amandus was bishop of Bordeaux around the year 400. He founded monasteries and preached throughout Flanders, making such a significant contribution to the new religion that he became known as "The Apostle of the Belgians."

Saint Bavo was a nobleman from Brabant who, when his wife died, gave away all his possessions and became a monk at Ghent. He did a great deal of missionary work in France and Flanders and then became a hermit.

Saint Bernard was born in France and on the death of his mother joined the Cistercians. With a few followers, he founded Cistercian monasteries that were to have a great influence in Belgium. Bernard laid down very strict rules that repelled some people, but many others were attracted to the new order. As the number of Cistercian monasteries grew, Saint Bernard became a very influential figure, with popes and rulers consulting him on important political matters.

years ago. Belgium's first married Catholic preacher started work in 2005 in the village of Dave, but his case was unusual as he had converted from Protestantism and was not forced to abandon his wife and children.

Lay people also play an important part in running the church. Committed members of the congregation may help in some of the services by reading from the Bible or assisting with Holy Communion.

The art of making stained glass developed from the 13th century onward, and the examples in Belgian churches by masters such as Jean Haeck are considered some of the finest in the world.

PILGRIMAGE

Belgium's most important Catholic pilgrimage is to Scherpenheuvel, in Flemish Brabant, on the first Sunday of November. The story goes that some time in the early 16th century a shepherd was wandering in the fields near Scherpenheuvel when he found a statue of the Virgin and Christ Child attached to an oak tree. When he tried to remove the statue, he became fixed to the ground. This was taken as a sign that the statue wished to remain there, and a chapel was built to house it. Although the statue was later destroyed, the place remained an important pilgrimage site, and kings often went to pray there before going into battle.

In 1933, in the tiny hamlet of Banneux near Liège, young Mariette Beco supposedly saw eight visions of the Virgin Mary. The village has since become a place of pilgrimage. The visions are very controversial, though, as some people think that the claim of the encounter was made to boost the income of the Beco family, who still run local gift shops.

Saint Hubert, a little town in the center of the Ardennes, is a pilgrimage site particularly popular with hunters. According to legend, Saint Hubert was hunting there when he saw a stag with a shining cross hanging between its antlers. A voice told him to take up missionary work, and he eventually became the Bishop of Liège. Today Saint Hubert is the patron saint of hunters.

Sick people might still make pilgrimages to the cathedral at Halle, a small city south of Brussels, which has a black Madonna statue that is believed to work miracles for people who pray before it.

LIVING MUSEUMS

Over the years, a great deal of energy has gone into building and decorating Belgium's churches and cathedrals. Today these religious sanctuaries are

guardians of a considerable part of Belgium's national heritage. Although primarily religious buildings, they are also recognized as cultural centers that house different forms of expression. Many treasures from the very earliest days of Christian history have been lost, but a few wonderfully handwritten Bibles, some decorated in ivory and gold, have survived.

The 1400s were noted for the great works of Flemish artists, many of which were commissioned for churches. Probably the most wonderful example is *The Adoration of the Lamb*, painted by Jan and Hubert van Eyck for the Cathedral of Saint Baaf in Ghent. The Antwerp Cathedral has a later but equally impressive treasure in two magnificent paintings by Peter Paul Rubens. Great numbers of church treasures were destroyed during the Reformation by fanatical Protestants. These Protestants are remembered as iconoclasts because they burned icons, which they considered to be signs of the church's forgetting of Christ's true message. The Saint Leonarduskerk in Zoutleeuw is the only major church interior in Belgium to have retained its full medieval splendor to this day.

Beautifully decorated churches are often put to good use for concerts of both religious and lay music. Pieces that feature wind instruments, such as trumpets, clarinets, horns, and organs, are particularly effective for the quality of the sound in the vaulting of Gothic cathedrals.

77

LANGUAGE

BELGIUM'S DEFINING FEATURE is its linguistic split between the Flemings (Flemish speakers) in the north and the Francophones (speakers of French) in the south. There is also a small German-speaking minority in eastern Belgium, near the German border.

THE LANGUAGE BARRIER

Long before the modern country of Belgium was created, this small area of Europe was already divided between the two language groups. Frankish tribes speaking a Germanic language settled in the north of the country, while Celts fled to the south, where their language was latinized as they were incorporated into the Roman Empire. The language division continues to this day. Language and politics have always been inextricably linked in Belgium.

At different times, each community has tried to force its language on the other, always resulting in trouble and much conflict.

When the Burgundian nobles rose to power, French became the language of the court and, therefore, of government and power. During the Dutch Revolt, Flanders tried to break away from Spanish-Catholic control along with fellow Dutch-speaking Holland, but was unsuccessful. Three centuries later, when Belgium briefly joined the Netherlands, William I attempted to impose Dutch as the official language on all the Belgians. It proved to be a bad mistake that ended in general rebellion.

A new constitution, signed in 1831, promised linguistic equality, but in practice it was a great advantage to speak French. Not only did French speakers have the best jobs, the language was also thought of as being more refined. On the contrary, Flemish was considered the language of

Above: **From 1814 onward, King William I ruled over the Dutch-speaking Netherlands, consisting of the present-day Netherlands, Belgium, and Luxembourg. Belgium became independent in 1830.**

Opposite: **The different linguistic divisions in Belgium are often reflected in the materials sold in bookshops around the country.**

farmers and laborers. As a result, many middle-class people of Flemish background chose to speak French to gain social advantages. This trend was reflected in the education system, as all lessons above primary level were conducted in French.

The revival of Flemish was stimulated by Hendrik Conscience and his inspiring book *The Lion of Flanders*, which was published in 1838. It demonstrated that Flemish could be a powerful literary language and it launched the campaign for *taalvrijheid* (TAAHL-vreye-heyet), meaning the freedom of language and the right to use Flemish in official dealings and education. Laws passed in 1898 gave both languages equal status. Nevertheless, as the country industrialized, much of Belgium's economic activity was based in French-speaking Wallonia, adding yet more power to the French part of the country.

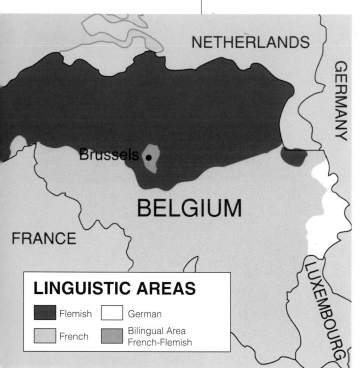

LINGUISTIC AREAS

Flemish   German
French   Bilingual Area
           French-Flemish

The use of the three official languages in Belgium is dictated by the linguistic areas in which the country has been divided.

Until quite recently, French was the main language of commerce, politics, and management. This meant also that one usually had to speak French to get the best jobs, even if one lived in the Flemish part of the country.

The German occupation of Belgium in 1940 triggered a few Flemish groups to campaign for a separate country under German protection, provoking considerable anti-Flemish feelings after the war. At that time, Belgium was forming far closer political links to France.

The 1960s brought the language question back as a prime issue. An official language frontier was formed in 1962, but the Flemings, believing

In the 1960s, violent demonstrations held between the Flemings and the French-speakers in Brussels prompted the government to find a solution to the severe problem of the language divide in a bid to avoid a brewing civil war.

they were still at a disadvantage, became more determined and occasionally violent in their protests. In 1968 students in the Flemish city of Leuven marched to demand that more classes be given in Flemish rather than French at the country's top university. The marches escalated into riots and eventually caused the Francophone part of the university to separate and move to Wallonia.

To resolve the never-ending linguistic problems, Belgium decided to form French, Flemish, and German communities to oversee cultural affairs within their regions. The different language regions acquired considerable autonomy from the central government and many of the past prejudices have now been addressed.

Still, language remains a major issue in Belgium today, and some people even think the language question could eventually split the nation into two. The Flemish daily newspaper *De Standaard* predicted, "It may take a decade, or a generation, but the Belgium state is dissolving itself." Flanders seems increasingly prepared for such an outcome and many of its inhabitants consider themselves Flemish rather than Belgian. In Wallonia, the French-speaking citizens still think of themselves as Belgian but are starting to realize that the country might indeed be split one day. If there were a split, a big dilemma would arise as the country wonders what to do with bilingual Brussels. There, a majority of people speak French, but the city is surrounded by Flanders.

A teenage boy does a live advertisement for a Flemish newspaper during the summer holidays at the Belgian coast.

SPOKEN AND WRITTEN LANGUAGES

For all practical purposes, written Flemish is the same as Dutch (Nederlands), the West Germanic language spoken in the Netherlands. But spoken Flemish has several very strong dialects that even the Dutch or other Flemish speakers will find relatively difficult to understand. One interesting difference is that the Dutch have adopted more English and French words into their vocabulary, particularly for technical subjects. In contrast, Flemish tends to create more distinctively Dutch terms to avoid incorporating French words.

Correct Belgian French is about as close to France's French as British English is to American English. To French ears, Belgian French produces a somewhat comical, throaty sound, while most Belgians find the sound of Parisian French painfully arrogant. However, the two forms of French are mutually intelligible, and Belgians happily watch a considerable quantity of television programs from France. French people find it harder to understand Belgian Francophones, especially if they start to add words from the Walloon (wah-LOHN) dialect.

Brussels is in a unique position. Officially it is a bilingual city, which means that city bureaucrats are expected to be fluent in both Flemish and French. In practice French or even English is much more widely understood in the city than Flemish. Some Brussels residents speak a blend of French and Flemish known as Bruxellois, the most marked form of which is called Marollien. This throws in words from the Spanish and Yiddish languages.

ACCENTS AND DIALECTS

Historically, Belgium was a collection of city-states, resulting in the wide range of local accents and dialects that vary not only from province to province but also from town to town and sometimes even from village to village. Belgians can easily tell where one comes from by his or her accent and dialect. Some accents and dialects are very distinctive and very hard to understand.

In the tourist areas of Belgium, signs advertise in Flemish, French, German, and English.

In Flanders the strongest accents are probably those of Limburg, Aalst, and Ostend. Some Flemish speakers find them difficult to understand. In Wallonia the Liège and Namur accents are also quite distinct and are often used for comic effect when telling jokes. The accents remain an active part of Belgian culture, although some of the most extreme versions are now dying out.

In Wallonia a series of local French dialects of Latin origin and influenced by the Celtic and Germanic languages are collectively known as Walloon. The three main forms of Walloon are almost mutually unintelligible and French speakers need a translator to understand them. All Walloon speakers, though, also understand Belgian French and can speak it, too, albeit often with a very heavy accent. Walloon usage is diminishing, but the language is still used in folkloric events and dialect-based literature and drama.

LANGUAGE AND DAILY LIFE

The language split has many practical implications for Belgian life. There are separate television and radio stations broadcasting in Flemish, French, and German. Newspapers address the different communities in their respective languages. So do ministers and other public figures during official functions. Belgian hospitals, schools, and police forces use one of the three languages, depending on their location in the country.

Belgian road signs can be very confusing for foreigners. That is because many town names are very different in French and Flemish. Things are easy enough in Brussels because road signs are bilingual. In Wallonia, however, directions on signposts are in French, even for Flemish towns. So to head for the town of Kortrijk, for example, signs to Courtrai need to be looked for instead. Similarly, signs in Flanders are in Flemish even for Francophone towns. A sign pointing to Bergen will lead you to the Francophone city of Mons. Some names are easy to identify in either language: Ath is Aat; Lier is Lierre; and Enghien is Edingen. However, some are very different indeed: Liège is Luik; Ronse is Renaix; Jodoigne is Geldenaken; and Jezus-Eik is Notre-Dame-au-Bois! The problem even extends to towns in neighboring countries: Lille in French is called Rijsel in Flemish, while Aachen in Germany is called Aix-la-Chapelle in French.

The language question seldom causes serious problems between individuals on a personal level. A Fleming caught speeding in Wallonia is probably going to be treated just the same as a French speaker. Whether or not they receive a fine or just a warning will depend on all kinds of factors, but language will probably not be a major influence. Tensions are worse in Flemish towns like Overrijse on the Brussels periphery, where Flemish people fear being swamped by non-Flemish speakers who have been moving into the area in recent decades. In certain places such as

NAMES

At first glance Belgian surnames appear to be clues to the part of the country people come from. It is a reasonable guess that anybody with a name like *van Damme* or *De Wilde* is from the northern, Flemish part of the country. Similarly, *Delvaux* and *Lefevre* suggest a Walloon origin. However, there have been centuries of mixing and intermingling between the communities, so in reality it is almost impossible to actually associate one's name with one's origin accurately. Common surnames in Belgium include Janssens, Vermeulen, Lemaitre, Peeters, Bruyne, Dupont, and Roelants. Multibarreled French surnames, especially those including the term *de* (of) tend to suggest an aristocratic background.

It is usual for Belgian children to be given three Christian names, although only the first will generally be used. Middle names typically include Ghislain (for boys) or Ghislaine (for girls), after the saint, in Wallonia along with the names of the godfather or godmother. Most Christian names have both a Flemish version and a French version. For example, Jan and Piet in Flemish translate to Jean and Pierre in French. However, these are not translated in daily life. The versions are interchangeably used only for the names of saints, churches, and royalty.

In recent years television and popular public figures also have a considerable influence on new names, and there is a growing tendency to use anglicized or non-European names for the sake of originality.

Flemish communes, local councils have demanded that people pass a Flemish language test before being allowed to buy land. This has been challenged as a violation of international human rights standards.

THE BELGIAN POLYGLOTS

As a small multilingual country, it is natural for Belgians to speak a second or third language or even more.

It is required that all children in Belgium learn a second national language. German and English are the most popular third languages. English is important as a language of advanced study, and as Germany is both a close neighbor and a major trading partner, German is an important language of commerce. Generally, Flemings seem open to learning another language. They are certainly more likely to speak French than a person from Wallonia is to speak Flemish. The Flemings's learning of the English language is also helped by having television programs that are subtitled rather than dubbed in English. In Wallonia, most programs are dubbed into French.

ARTS

BELGIUM HAS AN ACTIVE and exciting art scene, and a new wave of young Belgian artists is creating headlines in areas such as dance, fashion design, and music. Yet it is somewhat misleading to speak of a Belgian culture in exactly the same way as one does about a Japanese or a Russian culture, because the work of most Belgian artists is influenced and determined by their Francophone or Flemish backgrounds. Moreover, many of the greatest Belgian artists worked long before Belgium was officially created.

Above: **Belgium's Princess Mathilde admires the artwork in a museum as she sits before Belgian artist James Ensor's largest and most famous canvas,** *Entrance of Christ into Brussels,* **painted in 1888.**

Opposite: **The opera house in Brussels has recently been revamped into a leading cultural center. It stages great operas and houses Anne Theresa De Keersmaeker's dance company, which is internationally known.**

Early in the last century, the work of artists such as the painter James Ensor and the composer César Franck started to inspire a national feeling, sometimes called *La Belgitude* (LAH behl-ji-TUU-duh). There was also a generation of writers who wrote in French but whose stories drew from the history and culture of Flanders. As the language question became more important, it started to have a major influence in the world of art. In the 1960s, the formation of separate ministries of education and culture widened the division between the Walloon and Flemish cultures.

Today, French-speaking Belgians tend to follow the trends of France. This is reflected in the books they read, the plays they watch, and the music they listen to. Many of Belgium's best French-speaking artists have moved to France, in particular Paris, where they find the art scene more stimulating. The Flemish-speaking community has always appeared more interested in forging its own cultural identity and is not particularly influenced by events in the Netherlands. Nevertheless, the proximity of the German and, notably, Anglo-Saxon cultures does lead to their influence on Flemish culture.

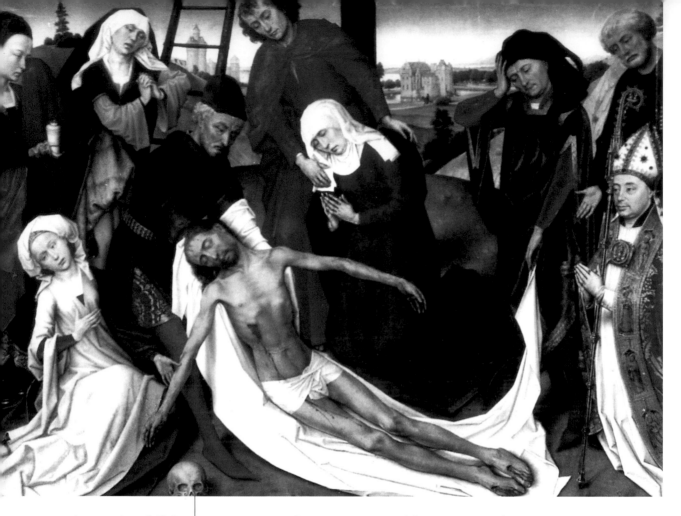

Lamentation of Christ by Rogier van der Weyden, founder of the Flemish movement in painting in the 15th century.

BELGIUM'S RICH CULTURAL PAST

Belgium has a rich artistic legacy. Until the 14th century, almost all art was commissioned by the church or nobility, and most paintings were either portraits or religious scenes, painted onto panels to decorate the altars in churches. As Flemish towns like Bruges developed, rich folk were increasingly able to commission portraits for themselves. Perhaps the most famous Flemish masters were the brothers Jan and Hubert van Eyck, who developed new techniques of oil painting that allowed them to add far more detail to their works than had been possible before.

Since cameras were not invented yet, ordinary folks started asking artists to include their homes and possessions in their portraits. Thus the art of landscape painting started to develop, initially as background. The van Eycks still worked on religious images and their *Adoration of the Lamb* (an altarpiece) is considered to be the greatest masterpiece of this period.

The second half of the 15th century is best remembered for the work of the Flemish painter Hans Memling. He settled in Bruges in 1465 and, despite the fact that the economy of the city was declining, managed to win important commissions. His paintings are admired for their beautiful detail.

The simmering religious revolution at the start of the 16th-century led several Flemish painters to follow the imaginative style of Dutch master Hieronymus Bosch (1450–1516). Bosch painted scenes of the afterlife with bizarre creatures inflicting terrible punishments on sinners. His work was really a form of surrealism, although it was to be several more centuries before that term would be first used.

The Peasant Wedding: Pieter Brueghel's impression of medieval rustic life in the Flemish countryside.

The last great Flemish master of this period was Pieter Brueghel the Elder (1525–69). He covered a wider range of subjects, including group portraits, landscapes, and still life. His pictures give an excellent idea of what life was like during this period. His famous painting *The Numbering of Bethlehem* shows Joseph and Mary on their donkey arriving at the inn, with the scene set in 16th century Flanders. Most of his canvases also contained strong social commentaries, which appealed to middle-class art buyers.

Within a generation, however, everything changed. While the newly independent Netherlands continued to develop secular art, encouraging the brooding genius of Rembrandt, the Dutch Revolts left Belgium suffering a drastic economic collapse. The only rich sponsor for art was the Catholic church. This led foremost 17th century Flemish masters like Peter Paul

The tapestry museum in Tournai. Skilled workers would take days to finish a few inches of a pattern.

Rubens to concentrate on producing vast canvases of angels and cherubs effectively glorifying the power and might of the church. Like many artists of the time, Rubens trained in Italy and produced an astonishing amount of work, ranging from giant altarpieces to portraits. Toward the end of his life Rubens retired to the countryside, where he painted landscapes for the first time.

Tapestry weaving flourished in the 15th and 16th centuries, and Belgium's large tapestries were considered to be the best in the world; they hung in palaces, churches, and noble homes all over Europe. The tapestries illustrated scenes from mythology, hunting, tales of chivalry, or Bible stories. The town of Oudenaarde specialized in "green" tapestries using patterns of leaves and plants.

Designs for tapestries were created by the best artists, and even Rubens once worked on a special design for the Vatican. Once the design was drawn, teams of five or six workers did the weaving, using colored yarns made from wool or silk. Gold and silver yarns were also used.

Belgian tapestries can be seen in museums around the country, and a special tapestry museum is located in Tournai (Doornik). The Royal Tapestry Manufacturers in Mechelen and some individual artists still keep the old skills alive.

MODERN PAINTERS

At the end of the 19th century the enigmatic Symbolist movement inspired painters such as Léon Spilliaert and the brilliant Fernand Khnopff, whose figures often appear in part-human, part-animal forms. Another very original painter was James Ensor, whose use of light, masks, and hybrid forms inspired many later artists.

The Surrealist movement had the strongest influence on modern Belgian painting, producing two world-famous modern painters, René Magritte and Paul Delvaux. Magritte's work is full of fascinating and strange ideas. Leaves turn into trees, trees into birds, and a gray mountainside is, at the same time, a great eagle. Probably his most famous canvas is a simple painting of a pipe, beneath which is written in French, "This is not a pipe."

Paul Delvaux was fascinated by trains and the Brussels trams. These often appear in his work as dark and sinister objects. Motionless nude figures with empty eyes form a common motif throughout Delvaux's work.

Each year, the Young Belgian Painting Group organizes a celebrated art fair with award-giving competitions for modern artists under 40. Promising artists are discovered there by well-known art galleries. Both the business community and the state are important sponsors of art. The state encourages artists by giving out grants to work on the facades of public buildings. The Brussels subway system is a famous example, with several stations each decorated by a different artist.

In his paintings, René Magritte experimented with a curious mixture of ordinary and strange images.

ARCHITECTURE

As well as religious masterpieces, the genius of medieval Belgian architecture is most apparent in the merchants' houses of Bruges and in fabulous soaring bell towers and trading halls that are found all across the country. These were a visible symbol of a town's wealth and independence and superb examples remain in Bruges, Saint Truiden, Lier, Ghent, and many other towns.

Belgian architecture came into its own again in the early 20th century, taking inspiration from the Art Nouveau movement. The totally new style used fluid spiral lines and natural curls, and was influenced by the Japanese, Celtic, and Turkish arts and the observation of nature. The strong sense for detail and beauty turned the movement into a highly decorative style. With architects Victor Horta and Henry van de Velde, Brussels once boasted the most beautiful Art Nouveau treasures in Europe. Tragically, careless monument protection policy and the demolition ball that tore through most cities in the 1960s and 1970s mean that relatively little of this heritage has survived.

Hôtel Tassel, designed by the architect Victor Horta, is one of the last examples of the more than 60 buildings that changed the architectural outlook of Brussels in the early 20th century.

MUSIC

As early as the 15th century, Belgium was famous for its choirs, which sang in four-part harmony. Belgian composers became famous in the princely churches and chapels of Rome, Milan, and Munich, and musicians came from all over Europe hoping to learn the secrets of the Flemish sound.

TWO FATHERS OF BELGIAN MUSIC

César Franck (1822–90)

César Franck was born in Liège, although he spent most of his musical career in Paris, where he worked as an organist and a professor at the Paris Conservatory. Franck produced a number of impressive compositions for piano, organ, and orchestra, as well as chamber music and religious oratorios. His use of a subtle counterpoint form gained him recognition as a modernizer of French music and one of the great composers of his time. His home city has opened a conservatory of music in his honor.

Adolphe Sax (1814–94)

Born in 1814, Adolphe Sax (*right*) worked in his father's musical instruments workshop in Dinant making flutes and clarinets. He was only 26 when he invented the first saxophone, a brass tube fitted with a single reed. Its sound was similar to a clarinet but deeper and more mellow. As the world of music was very conservative, Sax had trouble persuading people to take his new instrument seriously. But once it was accepted by the army band, it slowly grew in popularity, and it now has a special place in jazz and rock bands. Sax invented several other instruments, including the saxhorn, saxtuba, and the saxtromba.

As the Baroque style developed at the end of the 16th century, these Flemish musicians lost favor.

Belgian music took on a new life in the 19th century with composers César Franck and Peter Benoit. Under the influence of Benoit and of young composers, Flemish music schools in Brussels, Ghent, and Antwerp flourished.

Belgium does a great deal to encourage musicians. There are several major national competitions, as well as important international music festivals that include classical, jazz, and popular music. The world-reputed International Queen Elizabeth Contest focuses on performances by pianists, violinists, and vocalists and is held in alternating years. It attracts contestants from around the globe.

Belgians have a very international taste in pop music, with a strong preference for classic rock, blues, and a variety of new-age sounds. Francophone Belgians are keen followers of French pop, rap, and chanson singers, and are immensely proud that Jaques Brel, one of France's greatest all–time vocal legends, was in fact Belgian. Flanders produces a certain amount of polka-oompah music, but top Flemish groups tend to sing in English.

The linguistic tension that runs through Belgium has been a source of difficulty for many writers, but it has also provided the means for the nation to assert its identity.

LITERATURE

Literature, more than any other art form in Belgium, has been affected by the country's linguistic problems. Yet the two literary communities have followed similar paths even as they developed their individual characteristics and styles.

Flemish literature owes a great legacy to Guido Gezelle and Hendrik Conscience. Gezelle was born in Bruges in 1830. Writing poetry of great lyrical purity and of religious and Flemish nationalistic inspiration, this Flemish priest is considered one of the masters of modern European lyric poetry. It is said of Hendrik Conscience that he "taught his people to read." His story *The Lion of Flanders* (1838), said to be the first Flemish novel written, was characterized by Romantic inspiration and national consciousness.

At the beginning of the 20th century, a group of writers called *Van Nu en Straks* (Today and Tomorrow) published a review that hoped to gain more recognition in Europe for Flemish literature. Cyriel Buysse, Stijn Streuvels, and Herman Teirlinck were the major contributors. Many writers of the group were influenced by Guido Gezelle. During World War I young authors such as Felix Timmermans and Paul Van Ostaijen identified with the German Expressionist movement that was striving for peace and humanitarianism. Van Ostaijen turned later to the nihilistic Dada movement, which denied traditional artistic values.

Literature after World War II was characterized by novelists of different styles and influences, including the magic-realistic novels of Johan Daisne and Hubert Lampo, the socialist-existentialist novels of Louis Paul Boon, and new avant-garde groups. Among them, Hugo Claus became the predominant Flemish writer and is even considered a likely candidate for a Nobel Prize in literature. His novels, poems, and dramas often examine controversial subjects, such as collaboration with the Nazis during the war.

French-language Belgian authors have emerged from both communities. In 1867 Charles de Coster wrote *Thyl Uylenspiegel*, which demonstrated how French could have deep roots in Flanders's culture.

In 1881 Max Waller founded the movement called La Jeune Belgique, which attracted a group of young poets and novelists who were engaged in a search for identity: Camille Lemonnier, Eugène Demolder, Georges Virrès, and Georges Rodenbach. Soon a new generation of French-speaking Flemings played a key role in the history of Belgian writing with three poets of international renown: Émile Verhaeren, Max Elskamp, and Maurice Maeterlinck, who won the Nobel Prize in Literature in 1911 for his dramas. His *Pelléas et Mélisande* was arranged into a major opera by the French composer Claude Debussy.

Georges Simenon was a prolific author. He wrote some 400 books that inspired 54 movies and over 200 television plays. He passed away in 1989.

During and between the two World Wars, Belgian literature in French continued to flourish. Novels, poetry, and drama were characterized by stylistic experiments influenced by new and experimental techniques. Franz Hellens wrote fantastic and mysterious novels, Charles Plisnier's satyric novels won the French Prix Goncourt, and Clément Pansaers's subversive poetry linked the Paris and Zurich Dada movements. Interaction with the Paris literary scene was strong, and a number of Belgian writers moved to that city. So did Henri Michaux, one of the greatest poets of the 20th century. Georges Simenon is probably Belgium's best-known popular author, thanks to his great detective character, Maigret.

Women have always been prominent in Belgium's French language literature. Authors such as Marie Gevers, Suzanne Lilar, and Francoise Mallet-Joris expressed different literary styles in various genres from novels to essays. Marguerite Yourcenar was the first woman to be elected to the Académie Francaise. Since her spellbinding, if short, novel *Fear and Trembling*, Amélie Nothomb has become the latest star of French-Belgian literature.

FOREIGN WRITERS IN BELGIUM

Belgium, and particularly Brussels, has attracted many great foreign writers. Shakespeare studied in Antwerp. Much later Charlotte Brontë visited Brussels in 1842 to learn French. She later came back to work as a teacher, and her books *Villette* and *The Professor* give wonderful descriptions of old Brussels.

Lord Byron passed through to visit the battlefield of Waterloo. He is rumored to have vandalized one of the statues in Brussels's city center, and a minor financial scandal caused him to leave town rather quickly.

When exiled from France for supporting Napoleon III, Victor Hugo stayed several years in Brussels while working on *Les Misérables*. Karl Marx lived in Brussels from 1844, also after being expelled from Paris.

Perhaps the most famous Belgian character to appear in any book is the fictional detective Hercule Poirot. His character was created by the English author Agatha Christie.

CINEMA

Belgian cinema has enjoyed a certain renown for tackling weighty issues. Many films are more thought-provoking than entertaining. André Delvaux, probably Belgium's most famous filmmaker, directed his films in both Flemish and French, and adapted novels of Flemish and Belgian-French origin. Stijn Coninckx was nominated for an Oscar in 1993 for his social drama *Daens*, filmed in Flemish. Of Francophone filmmakers, Belgium's most successful are the brothers Luc and Jean-Pierre Dardenne. They achieved the extremely rare accolade of winning the Cannes Palme d'Or twice with *Rosetta* (1999) and *L'Enfant* (2005). Chantal Akerman's French-language films are also much admired. Among filmgoers rather than critics, the most popular Belgian film was probably Jaco van Dormael's *Le Huitième Jour* about a Down syndrome sufferer.

Belgium's most internationally famous film star is the martial arts actor Jean-Claude Van Damme. Nicknamed "Muscles from Brussels," Van Damme is probably the most instantly recognized Belgian face in Asia and the United States. Few people realize that screen idol Audrey Hepburn was born in Brussels.

DRAMA AND DANCE

Belgian theater and dance companies have a reputation for staging excellent productions. Many of the companies perform extensively abroad and have won international awards. Theatrical life in Belgium today is blooming with an increasing number of high-quality companies. Theater and dance festivals, which stage local and international companies, enjoy high attendance.

Theaters in Brussels and Wallonia stage the work of playwrights such as Maurice Maeterlinck, Michel de Ghelderode, Suzanne Lilar, and contemporary writers Liliane Wouters and Jean-Marie Piemme.

Wim Vandekeybus's company at work. His fascinating performances include dancers, blind actors, and live music.

A major international repertoire has also been adapted, from Samuel Beckett and Dario Fo to William Shakespeare.

Flemish theater production is most influenced by the work of playwright, poet, and novelist Hugo Claus, who also directed the theater group in his hometown of Ghent.

In addition, strong local actors and directors have searched for new forms of expression that have led some companies to make links between theater, dance, and film. The internationally known works of Jan Fabre and Wim Vandekeybus are examples of the new forms.

For almost three decades the Brussels opera, Théâtre de la Monnaie, was home to Maurice Béjart's *Ballet du XXème Siècle* (though it has since moved to Lausanne, Switzerland). Béjart, long a symbol of the modern

CARTOONS

Second only to Japan, Belgium is the home of cartoon books. These are considered works of art and are by no means exclusive to children. The most internationally famous is Tintin, the young reporter, with his dog, Snowy, and his friend, Captain Haddock. Created by cartoonist Hergé, Tintin first appeared in newspapers in 1929 in an adventure called *Tintin in the Land of the Soviets*. Since then his adventures have taken him all over the world and even to the moon. In Belgium and much of Europe, Tintin is as famous as Garfield is in the United States. In fact, General Charles de Gaulle, the late president of France, once said Tintin was the only figure in the world more famous than he was!

Other famous Belgian cartoons include Spirou, Marsupilami, and Lucky Luke. Spirou is a hotel bellboy who has a series of exciting and comical adventures. Lucky Luke is a cowboy with a faithful horse, Jolly Jumper, and Marsupilami is a strange spotted animal from outer space.

Cartoon and animation films have also been successful in the Belgian and international film industries. The rather earthy but very humorous films by Brussels's humorist Picha have been screened all over the world, and Raoul Servais and Nicole van Goethem, from Ghent and Antwerp, respectively, have won several international awards.

Belgian dance scene, is known worldwide. His ballet school, Mudra, has revived the Belgian dance tradition and trained many dancers and choreographers. Under Béjart's influence and in reaction to his style, other young advocates of modern dance, such as Anne Theresa De Keersmaeker and Michèle Anne Demey, have made their marks on international stages.

FAMOUS LACE MAKING

Lace making is a classic Belgian craft. The tradition is especially strong in Brussels and the surrounding Brabant countryside. Lace first became popular in the 16th century when rich men and women wore it to decorate their clothing and to flaunt their wealth.

Brussels lace was particularly prized, as it was finely made and used interesting designs. At the height of the fashion for lace in the 17th and 18th centuries, the industry employed thousands of women, giving them an important source of income.

Professional lace makers are trained from childhood and produce the finest designs following traditional patterns.

The economic importance of lace making became quite a political issue. At one point the British government became worried about how much money was being spent on Belgian lace, and they tried to ban its import. Emperor Philip II of Belgium sought to prevent girls over the age of 12 from working in the industry. It was attracting so many of them that it had become difficult to find anybody willing to work as servants. Neither ruler had much success with these campaigns. Eventually wearing lace simply went out of fashion.

Today tourism and a growing interest in the past have revived lace making, and many Belgian women have started learning and practicing the art, both as a hobby and as a source of extra income. Most of the lace, usually used for tablecloths and blouses, finds its way to tourist shops in Bruges and Brussels. Because of the work involved and the high cost of labor in Belgium, lace is expensive. A large tablecloth can cost anywhere from $250 to $700, depending on its quality and detail.

LEISURE

WITH A FIVE-DAY WORKWEEK of 38 hours, some 10 official holidays, and 20 days paid vacation, leisure time in Belgium amounts to nearly 150 days a year. That allows Belgians to indulge in many leisure activities.

GETTING OUTDOORS

Belgians are great sun worshippers. Because the weather tends to be gray and cold, people like to head outdoors whenever it is sunny and warm, and barbecues are extremely popular among those with backyards of their own.

Belgians love to catch up with each other over a drink at the local café or pub, where time is also spent listening to popular music or playing games. Certain cafés offer card and board games, chess, and variants of billiards and pool. Some offer appealing outdoor terraces.

Art lovers enjoy an extensive selection of museums and art galleries throughout the country, and great art exhibitions are organized in the major cities. During special exhibitions and carnivals, the Belgian railway company often offers special travel packages.

Once a year, on the occasion of the Open Monuments Day, a selection of private and official buildings in Belgium open their doors to the public, allowing art and architecture lovers to view treasures that are normally hidden away. In the suburbs around the major cities, big new cinema complexes show the latest local and international movies.

Above: **The Belgian coast attracts tourists in any season.**

Opposite: **A group of Belgian youngsters enjoy the sun at Parc de Leken.**

HOBBIES

Belgians enjoy a whole range of hobbies. The bigger cities have shops catering to the needs of stamp collectors, model makers, and toy-train collectors, as well as numerous pet stores. Many Belgians are keen collectors who like hunting in antiques dealers' shops and at numerous outdoor markets, notably in Brussels's Sablon area and in Tongeren on Sundays.

Many towns also have sports clubs, cultural circles, choirs, amateur theater groups, brass bands, youth clubs, senior citizens' clubs, and political groups. Even small towns generally have a cultural center with occasional performances, travel lectures, and concerts. Gardening is a very popular pastime for people living in suburbs or villages.

Classic antique cafés like the La Chaloupe d'Or/De Gulden Boot on Brussels's wonderful Grand Place, are the ideal place to savor Belgium's excellent coffee or world-class beers.

Many Belgians have a soft spot for pets, with cats, dogs, and birds being the favorites. Tanks with tropical fish decorate many living rooms. Caged birds of various species can be purchased in markets.

VACATIONS

During short holidays and weekends, the population is quick to rush off to the sandy North Sea beaches or to go hiking and skiing in the hilly

Ardennes. There are no permanent ski resorts because the snow is too unpredictable, but cross-country enthusiasts abound.

Belgium has its own amusement and theme parks, which include water parks, zoos, and safari parks. It is possible to boat calmly along Belgium's extensive canal system and inland waterways, ride old steam trains, or explore caves in the Ardennes.

Longer vacations are more likely to be taken abroad, not just because there is a better chance of enjoying sunshine but also because it often works out cheaper than vacationing at the Belgian coast. In 2005, 69 percent of Belgians vacationed away from home at least once. The most popular foreign getaway destinations were France, Spain, Turkey, Greece, Egypt, and Tunisia.

TELEVISION

Television broadcasting in Flanders is completely separate from that in Wallonia. Belgium has one of the most extensive systems of cable television in the world.

Special pet markets, held on Sundays, make it hard for visitors to resist the charm of cuddly puppies and kittens.

With roughly 90 percent of its households having access to cable channels, the average family receives not just Belgian programming but also a selection of productions from other nations, typically France, the Netherlands, the United Kingdom, Germany, Portugal, Italy, and Spain, along with European CNN, MTV, and Euro News channels. However, despite these choices, most cable operators in Wallonia do not offer more than one Flemish channel. Similarly, in Flanders a viewer is as likely to obtain broadcasting from France in French as from Wallonia.

Being a small nation with a limited audience means that Belgian television cannot afford to produce many television dramas of its own and therefore must import shows from other countries. The French region naturally favors programs made in France, but both areas telecast programs from Britain and the United States. In Flemish areas, these will generally be shown in English with subtitles. In Wallonia, the programs are usually dubbed into French.

Radio is still very popular. People typically tune in to their favorite station in the mornings, and especially when driving , if only for warnings about traffic delays and police speed checks. It is not at all unusual to have the radio playing quietly in factories and cafés. There are dozens of radio stations divided by language, region, and theme. Specialist stations cater to minority groups, including Italian and Turkish speakers.

GAMBLING

The most popular forms of gambling are operated by the national lottery, which has various games such as LOTTO and Joker and popular instant-win scratch cards. All are available from special booths found on street corners or in bigger supermarkets.

Since 1984, the small Walloon village of Redu has developed as Belgium's book village. It currently has 39 bookshops plus several art galleries, cafés, and workshops specializing in papermaking, printing, and bookbinding. Once a year, Book Weekend attracts hundreds of book lovers and secondhand book dealers, who set up stalls along the streets. Every August a Book Night culminates in fireworks.

Urban Belgians lining up to buy lottery tickets.

Slot machine gambling is not permitted in bars or cafés. Many towns have minicasinos, which are more often small shops than grand Las Vegas-style palaces.

In many cafés one can find a game called Den Tosch. This looks somewhat like a pinball machine or Japanese pachinko. A spring-loaded button fires balls onto a slope. The balls fall into numbered holes, and certain combinations win the player credits to play again. These credits can often be (illegally) resold to the café owner for cash.

CYCLING

Cycling is the national sport of Belgium. There is a strong network of clubs where members train together for competitions. The Tour of Belgium is considered one of the top events on the professional

Paths along Belgium's canals are free of automobile traffic and are ideal tracks for amateur or professional cyclists. However, riding on public roads can be hazardous.

cycling calendar. However, nothing in the sport compares with the excitement of the Tour de France, which often passes through Belgium at some stage to let Belgian racing fans enjoy the spectacle. Belgian cyclists have a good record in the event—one of the most famous cyclists of all time is Belgian Eddy Merckx, who won the Tour de France five times.

Thousands of locals go cycling in the countryside every weekend, and they view this as much of a social occasion as a sporting competition. In Flanders many locals keep an old "boneshaker" for making short trips around town, and there are considerable networks of cycle paths. Several touring circuits have been set up around the country, notably the Vlaanderen route, which covers a distance of 398 miles (640 km).

Most of Belgium is flat, which makes cycling easy and popular. However, especially in Wallonia, cycling on public roads can be hazardous due to inconsiderate driving.

SOCCER

Extremely popular with Belgian men, soccer is played at all levels and by all age groups. In the villages, the soccer team is often an important part of the local social life. Dances and other events organized by the community help to raise a little money to run the team.

The first international soccer match in continental Europe was held in Belgium. Belgium's national soccer squad, nicknamed the Red Devils, is now considered to be one of the few positive symbols of a unified Belgium and is supported by Flemish and Francophone Belgians alike. The team, however, did not even manage to reach the main qualifying stages of the 2006 World Cup. At the professional club level Belgium has a strong league that plays games on Saturday evenings or Sunday afternoons supported by enthusiastic fans. Football Club Brugge and Football Club Anderlecht are the most famous clubs. Teams are free to employ foreign players as Beveren did to great effect in 2003 when essentially buying a whole team from the African nation of Ivory Coast.

Soccer is extremely popular among Belgian men.

OTHER SPORTS

The remarkable success of Kim Clijsters and Justine Henin has suddenly thrust tennis into the forefront of Belgian sporting interest. Professional basketball also has a considerable following, notably at Charleroi. Brussels organizes an annual marathon and has "Roller Days" where sections of town are briefly shut down for a swarm of roller skaters to whiz through.

Motor sports are popular. Until being cancelled in 2006 following a financial scandal, the Belgian Grand Prix Spa-Francorchamps course was frequently said to be the favorite for drivers. Belgium's most famous Formula One stars were Thierry Boutson and Jacky Ickx.

Belgium has over 50 golf clubs. The Royal Antwerp Club was founded in 1888, making it one of the oldest in the world. Golf was introduced by British workers who came to Belgium in the 19th century to help build railways and factories. The French pastime of pétanque (peh-TAHNK), a subdued bowling game generally played outdoors, has a fairly strong following in Wallonia.

Some Belgian stables are well known for their excellent horses, which are trained very seriously and participate in races and equestrian shows. Many people simply enjoy riding along the coasts or in the forests.

PIGEON RACING

Belgium, along with the north of England, can claim to be the founder and home of pigeon racing. Many special species of racing pigeons have been bred around Antwerp, and Belgium founded the international body that governs the sport.

Pigeon racing is particularly strong in the rural regions and is very much a male–dominated activity. Although it is seen mostly as an activity for older people, many men teach the sport to their sons. The *duivenmelker* (DEUY-vuhn-mehl-kuhr), or pigeon racer, plans the breeding program in the hope of producing champions, trains pigeons for the big events, and bets on them as well.

Races are governed by strict rules. The pigeons are handed over to the race officials in the hometown and taken away to be released together. Races generally start over short distances and get longer as the season progresses. By the end of a racing year, the birds might be taken as far as southern France before being released to find their way back. They usually fly at 40 miles (64 km) per hour, but if there is a strong wind behind them, they can go much faster. When the pigeons are due to arrive home, the nervous owner tries to keep everybody in the house quiet, as pigeons may not land if they are alarmed by any noise. As soon as a pigeon lands, a ring is removed from its foot and placed into a special time clock that records the finishing time for the bird. The sealed clock is taken to the club headquarters, where the pigeon racer finds out how his champion bird has performed against its rivals. Half the fun of pigeon racing comes from the social aspect of the competition, and most owners spend the afternoons in discussion with fellow racers.

FESTIVALS

BELGIUM'S NATIONAL HOLIDAYS fall on New Year's Day (January 1), Labor Day (May 1), Easter Monday (dates vary), the country's very own National Day (July 21), Assumption (August 15), All Saints (November 1), Armistice Day (November 11), and Christmas Day (December 25). In addition, each linguistic community has a regional holiday. Belgium's unique carnivals and processions are the biggest celebrations in the country even though they are not official holidays. Some are very colorful occasions when hundreds of people dress up in amazing costumes.

Above: **Belgian children visit Santa Claus (*Sinterklaas* or Saint Nicholas) who checks whether they have been good before deciding if they deserve a present.**

Opposite: **Young boys and girls in colorful costumes during the Procession of the Golden Tree.**

CHRISTMAS

Christmas is an important celebration in Belgium as it is with most Christian countries. Pretty lights and decorations add character to townscapes. Schools close for a two-week-long vacation, although most workers get only one day's statutory holiday. Belgian children effectively get to enjoy two Christmases. The first set of presents arrives on Saint Nicholas Day (December 6). Children will leave out socks or boots expectantly and hope to find them filled by Saint Nicholas, or *Sinterklaas*, the Belgian Santa Claus. It is typical to leave a carrot for Santa's donkey—in Belgium Santa does not use Rudolf the Red-nosed Reindeer. December 6 is not a holiday, but it is a tradition to eat specially formed *speculoos* (gingerbread cookies) on that day. Saint Nicholas often appears in shopping centers or special festive markets in Belgium, usually accompanied by a man with

At Christmastime, most towns and cities set up impressive decorations in the main square.

an artificially blackened face. This mysterious stick-wielding figure is called Black Peter. It is supposedly Black Peter's job to check that children have been good enough to deserve their presents.

On the evening of Christmas Eve (December 24) family members enjoy a special dinner together. Many families, even those who do not usually attend church, might attend the Midnight Mass on Christmas Eve. Christmas Day (December 25) is often a time to visit relatives, and lunch is the main meal of the day. On Christmas Day everybody, not just the children, exchanges presents.

NEW YEAR

New Year's Eve has far less tradition attached to it and is simply a time to go out and enjoy oneself. This might mean attending a party or dining at a restaurant. Toward midnight people often gather in the town center to welcome the new year together. Many towns give a spectacular display of fireworks at midnight.

NATIONAL AND COMMUNITY HOLIDAYS

Belgium's National Day is celebrated on July 21. It commemorates the day King Leopold I took his oath as monarch. There are celebrations throughout the country and a military parade in Brussels. Vielesam's blueberry festival is held the same day. It is preceded on the evening before by a remarkable "capture" of the little town by "Macralle witches" who then put on a show in thick Walloon dialect.

Each linguistic community has its own principal holiday. On July 11 the Flemish community celebrates the anniversary of the Battle of the Golden Spurs. The French community day falls on September 27, commemorating the day patriots in Brussels enjoyed a victory over the Dutch in 1830. The German-speaking community celebrates its national day on November 15.

Armistice Day, November 11, is the day in 1918 that World War I came to an end, but the national holiday commemorates those who died in all wars since. The day means more to older people who remember the world wars. Special services are conducted at the sites of battlefields, and flowers are placed at war monuments. Churches hold memorial services for those who died for their country, and old soldiers proudly don their uniforms again.

A Belgian in the costume of a soldier during the celebration of the Battle of the Golden Spurs which took place in 1302.

BINCHE, THE CARNIVAL TOWN

The little town of Binche in southern Belgium lives for its carnival, a yearly celebration that can be traced back to the 14th century. The key figures are the Gilles (JEEH-luh), clowns wearing wooden clogs and bright, colorful medieval costumes stuffed with straw and decorated with heraldic lions. Bells hang from their belts, jangling as they make a curious shuffling dance to the sound of brass bands and drums. Being a Gille is considered a great honor, which is passed on from father to son.

The carnival has two climaxes. The first occurs at around 11 A.M. when groups of Gilles converge on the central square. They then put on spooky masks before entering the beautiful city hall building. In the afternoon there is a more formal procession. This time the Gilles wear high hats with enormous plumes of ostrich feathers (if it is not too windy) and throw oranges into the crowd from special baskets. Oranges are sometimes thrown so hard that some Binche residents board up their windows for protection. However, if spectators are hit, it is considered a wondrous, albeit painful, blessing. Throwing oranges back again would be considered extremely offensive. The festival ends with a giant bonfire and considerable public intoxication as everybody drinks beer throughout the day—legal on Belgian streets as it is in New Orleans.

CARNIVALS AND OTHER EVENTS

Belgium has some of the world's most fascinating carnivals. Although carnivals traditionally fall on Mardi Gras, the Tuesday before Lent—the forty days before Easter—somewhere in Belgium there is at least one carnival held virtually every weekend from January until Easter itself. In certain towns carnivals are the most important events in the people's year, and various voluntary groups work together to organize street parades. The most famous and distinctive are held at Stavelot (the fourth Saturday of Lent) with its Blancs Moussis (characters wearing long-nosed masks) and especially at Binche (on Mardi Gras) featuring the extraordinary Gilles. The day before Mardis Gras the German-speaking town of Eupen celebrates Rose Monday with an especially colorful carnival. The multiday carnival at Aalst has a unique if rather boisterous feel to it. It starts on Sunday with a procession of "giants," Monday sees onion-throwing parades, and the celebration ends with the hilarious "dirty aunts" parade, where most of the town's male population dress up in gaudy women's clothing.

EASTER CELEBRATION AND PROCESSIONS

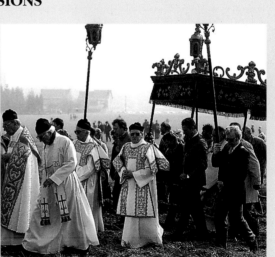

At Easter painted eggs are traditionally hidden in gardens for children to seek out. These days it is also common to send cards to friends and give chocolate eggs as gifts, much as in the United States. At Eastertime, churches see some of the largest congregations of the year. Small towns and villages have their own Easter parades, such as this one (*right*) in Hakendover. Among the strangest Easter parades is the Procession of Penitents. This occurs on the night of Good Friday in the Walloon town of Lessines. Participants march somberly around the darkened streets carrying heavy wooden crosses and dressed in cloaks with conical hoods.

The most famous Ascension Day parade is the Procession of the Holy Blood. This takes place in Bruges with hundreds of people dressed up as Biblical figures marching through the streets. At the center of the procession are the priests carrying a receptacle said to contain drops of Jesus's blood. On Trinity Sunday, Mons's classic Saint Wadru festival culminates with a Procession of the Golden Carriage and a fight between Saint George and the dragon. The Mons Saint George is actually dressed as a 17th-century cavalryman rather than a third-century knight. The battle represents the struggle between good and evil, but for spectators the fun is in the attempt to grab a hair from the dragon's long tail.

HISTORICAL PARADES

Some of Belgium's parades and festivals are reenactments of historic events. The most famous celebration in Brussels is the *Ommegang* (OHM-muh-gang) in July, which is modeled on a parade staged before Charles V in 1549. In the evening, more than 2,000 of the city's residents dress up in medieval costumes and parade around the city and into the Grand Place. The parade includes horse riders, stilt walkers, jesters, soldiers, aristocrats, and finally the imperial family and their court. Even Manneken Pis joins in the celebration and is dressed in a special festival costume.

Bruges has a medieval parade called the Procession of the Golden Tree that takes place only once every five years. It stages a stylized reenactment of the 1468 wedding of Charles the Bold and Princess Margaret of York.

During the *Ommegang*, the center of Brussels is closed to traffic to allow the parade to pass through the streets.

Ieper (Ypres) is famous for the Festival of Cats, which dates back to the Middle Ages and the belief that cats were associated with the devil. To disprove this idea, Count Baudouin had all the cats taken to the tower of the town hall and thrown off to show they were not immortal. This bloody and bizarre spectacle went on until the 19th century. Today only soft toys are thrown from the tower. The festival also has a magnificent parade with bands, medieval costumes, and, of course, giant cats.

In August giant figures, some 13 feet (4 m) tall, parade through the town of Ath. The huge figures are carried by one or two people hidden inside. The French character of the town is reflected in the parade. The giants, with their costumes of red, white, and blue, often look like Napoleon's soldiers. The highlight of the parade is a reenactment of the fight between David and Goliath.

SEASONAL FESTIVALS

While May 1 (Labor Day) is celebrated by many with socialist banners and red flags, in Belgium it is primarily a day when men present small posies of lilies of the valley to female colleagues, friends, and family members.

In late spring some towns, notably Brussels and Ghent, deck their main squares with a magnificent carpet of petals from a wide variety of fresh flowers.

From May to September, several marches have people dressed up in old military uniforms and marching to the sound of bands, drums, pipes, and gunfire. Probably the oldest is Thuin's Saint Roch March, started as a religious appeal against a deadly plague. The famous Saint Rolende March covers over 20 miles (32 km) starting from Gerpinnes. The battles around Waterloo are commemorated most years with various groups dressed in Napoleonic costumes. Occasionally the whole battle is reenacted.

The marches probably date back to the 16th century when military escorts were provided when religious relics were transported from town to town. Today the marches are dedicated to the saints. They are wonderful social events and add another dimension to the country's pageantry.

The biggest marches can involve up to 5,000 people, as well as all their supporters and families. The Rolende March covers 20 miles (32 km) starting from Gerpinnes.

FOOD

THROUGHOUT BELGIUM'S TURBULENT HISTORY, its cuisine has absorbed culinary influences from both Latin and Germanic cultures. Traditionally, many Belgian recipes were heavy and rustic, but today the country's restaurants are famous for serving food of French quality in German-size portions. Whatever cuisine they choose, Belgians consider good dining as one of life's greatest pleasures.

Flemish Charles de l'Ecluse played an important role in introducing the potato throughout Europe, and potatoes remain at the heart of most traditional Belgian meals. A classic if less exotic local specialty is *stoemp*, boiled potatoes mashed with a seasonal vegetable and served with ham or sausage.

Many Belgian towns also have developed their own regional specialities. Liège was the original home to the *salade Liègeoise* (sah-LAH-duh lee-a-JWAH-zuh), which combines bacon, potatoes, onions, parsley, and green beans. The Liège region is also famous for stews and soups. Ghent has contributed the famous creamy *waterzooi* (WAH-tuhr-zoohj) soup once made from fish but now just as likely from chicken. Recipes vary wildly, but, at its best, this dish is rich and creamy, and simultaneously as refreshing as a clear soup. Brussels pioneered the art of cooking with beer, as well as making the world famous Belgian waffles. The Ardennes region is noted for game such as venison, boar, and partridge, while the North Sea provides Belgium's well-known mussels and gray shrimps.

Cooking in Belgium is strongly influenced by the availability of different foods with the changing seasons. Although the globalized supply chain now makes cultivating and harvesting seasons less important than in previous eras, people still eagerly wait for the *primeurs* (pree-MEUH-rs), or early vegetables and fruits of the season, for which times restaurants organize special gastronomic events. Herrings are best in spring, May and June bring fresh asparagus and juicy strawberries, and fall marks

Raw ingredients for the night's cooking are often displayed on a cart or table in front of a restaurant. A seafood display is first packed with ice, then lobsters, prawns, and crabs are carefully placed within a border of fresh vegetables. An enormous fish, its mouth gaping, forms a dramatic centerpiece. Artistically decorated boards advertise the speciality of the day.

Opposite: **An array of Belgian food on display.**

the start of the hunting season and the arrival of wild game in the shops. Mussels are best in winter.

MARKETS VERSUS SUPERMARKETS

The pattern of shopping in Belgium has changed drastically over the last 30 years. Small groceries, specialty shops, and markets used to be the only places that sold food and other supplies, but big supermarkets are taking more and more of the trade. Still, markets remain important as places where Belgians can find fresh food and flowers, and have an enjoyable day out. Markets are often held on Sundays, when the big malls are closed. Markets tend to be a colorful international blend, especially in cities with a high concentration of immigrants.

The Brussels Midi Market offers exotic delicacies from Italian pepper cheese and Turkish olives to African salted fish. Small stores in towns and villages offer convenience and special service. Local bakeries stock a daily range of fresh breads, rolls, pastries, and cakes. The local butcher offers all sorts of raw and cooked meats. The main street delicatessens tempt customers with displays of cold lunch meats, fish, salads, and cheeses that they will make into delicious French bread sandwiches upon request—an ideal quick and tasty lunch.

MEAT

Meat forms an important part of Belgian cuisine, and steak with french fries is probably the nation's favorite meal. Pork, rabbit meat, and chicken are also eaten regularly, and horse meat is traditionally considered a delicacy (though the number of specialist horse butchers is diminishing). Various cuts of meat can be made into old-style hot pots cooked in a casserole with beer or prunes. Lamb is relatively expensive but prized, while sweetbreads, kidneys, and goose liver are considered among the most mouthwatering of luxury foods. Belgians can choose from an amazing range of sausages, many seasoned with herbs and spices. Ham and pâté from the Ardennes and salami are also popular.

Ham, pâté, sausages, and other cooked meat products can be found in specialty shops.

Some hearty dishes are predominantly winter favorites, including *Vlaamse karbonade* (VLAAHM-suh khar-boh-NAH-duh), a tasty beef stew cooked in a special local beer. Other specialities include *faisan à la Brabanconne* (fuh-SAHN ah lah brah-bahn-SOH-nuh), pheasant braised with endive, and *konijn met pruimen* (koh-NEYHN meht PREU-muhn), rabbit cooked in beer with onions and prunes. *Ballekes* (BA-la kes), meatballs in tomato sauce, are less glamorous but remain a mainstay of traditional home cooking.

Fresh seafood is available throughout the country, and it is common to find oysters, lobster, and crayfish from the Belgian, Dutch, and French North Sea coasts.

SEAFOOD

Seafood is very popular in Belgium, and few sights are more typical than a group of diners in a seaside restaurant enjoying a steaming pot of mussels. Herbs are particularly important when cooking mussels, with onions, celery, and parsley creating that special Belgian flavor.

Belgium's North Sea gray shrimps are said to be the best in the world. A few fishers, in bright yellow oilskins, still catch these the traditional way that involves using strong Brabant horses to trawl a net through waist-high water. The most typical preparation is to boil the shrimps in salted water, shell them, and coat the flesh lightly with mayonnaise. They are then often served stuffed into a hollowed-out tomato.

Inland, river fish provide another Belgian delicacy, *paling in het groen* (PAH-ling ihn hut GROON), eel cooked in a bright green parsley sauce and served cold. Another favorite is *truite au bleu* (TRWEET oh bleuh), trout cooked with carrots, leeks, and potatoes, and most famously served in the idyllic Walloon village of Crupet. When the weather turns cold, street stalls around shopping areas or markets often sell freshly boiled snails in their shells as a winter warmer.

SPECIAL VEGETABLES

Few cities have a vegetable named after them, but Brussels sprouts are world famous. The first record of Brussels sprouts being eaten in Belgium dates to 1587, but they were probably part of the local diet three or four centuries earlier. Sprouts grow best in cool climates and are damaged by hot weather. An excellent source of vitamins A and C, sprouts are typically a winter favorite.

Particularly prized is the Belgian asparagus, eaten in Belgium since Roman times. People favor the thick white spears and their rich flavor. The best asparagus comes from the sandy soils of the region around Mechelen.

Witloof, or chicory (Belgian endive), is used in typical hearty winter dishes.

Witloof (WHIT-loohf), or chicory (Belgian endive), has not become so universally popular, but it is probably the best example of a Belgian vegetable. Belgians use both the leaves as a salad and the roots as a vegetable. As a vegetable, endive is usually diced, slightly sweetened, and boiled, or wrapped whole in slices of ham and cooked in a creamy cheese sauce. Other popular vegetables include red cabbages and leeks.

BELGIAN FRIETEN, BELGIAN FRITES

Although Americans know deep-fried potatoes as french fries, the Belgians and Britons both claim to have invented them. Known in Belgium as *frieten* (FREEH-tehn, in Flemish) or *frites* (FREEH-tuh, in French), fried potatoes are a favorite Belgian street food served from mobile canteens or small huts. They are handed to customers in paper cones or on small cardboard

The typical Belgian *frite*, eaten as a snack, is long and thick. A thinner variety, called lucifers, is served with fine Belgian dishes.

trays. Usually customers have them topped with a large dollop of flavored mayonnaise of which there is a bewildering variety.

Belgian *frites* have a delicious texture and flavor because they are fried twice in hot oil, first to cook the inside, then to brown and crisp the exterior. In restaurants they are served as the usual accompaniment to mussels or steak.

THE MEAL PATTERN

Even if the family has to get to school or work, breakfast still tends to be a surprisingly relaxed mealtime. People usually sit down together and take half an hour over the meal. Breakfast is generally light: rolls, croissants, pastries, or bread with jam or cheese, and perhaps an egg washed down with coffee, or perhaps some tea, milk, or hot chocolate.

Unlike in Spain and Italy, Belgium does not halt its activities for a long siesta at lunchtime. Although many restaurants offer special lunch menus, it is common for working Belgians to simply snack on a French-bread sandwich from a *traiteur* (tray-TER) or delicatessen.

Dinner is usually the main meal of the day. Although in restaurants Belgians typically display a wide range of tastes in and an appreciation for international cuisines, most home-cooked meals are relatively simple, consisting of potatoes with meatballs in tomato sauce, chicken with applesauce, or perhaps a simple spaghetti.

Atmosphere is very important for a good meal, and restaurants go to great trouble over the tableware, linen, and lighting.

Traditionally, Sunday lunch is the most important meal of the week. It is a time for the family and relatives to sit together in a relaxed atmosphere. Several dishes, desserts, and drinks may be served throughout the afternoon.

There is little that is different about a Belgian kitchen from a standard kitchen in the United States. However, a few items in the cutlery laid on the tables might surprise visitors, like the tiny forks for prying snails out of their shells.

DESSERTS

A nation with such great love for food is naturally going to be an expert when it comes to desserts. Some desserts are traditionally associated with towns or regions. For example, *kletskoppen* (KLEH-ts-koh-puhn), crunchy sweet cookies, originally came from Bruges, and *tarte al d'jote* (TAHRT ahl DJOH-tuh), a tart from Nivelles that is made of beet leaves and cheese. Ghent has special little cakes called *Gentse mokken* (GHENT-suh MOHK-kun), and Brussels contributes its famous Belgian waffles, served with sugar, butter, fresh cream, or fresh fruit, or both.

Belgium is home to hundreds of regional cheeses, some of which are produced in old monasteries that still use traditional methods. Even the country's most classic cheeses, such as Passendale, Maredsous, and the infamously smelly Herve, are virtually unheard of outside Belgium.

127

Belgian pralines are famous worldwide. Any shop assistant will happily make up an assorted collection to meet the taste of each customer.

Nationwide favorites include sugar tart, chocolate mousse, white cheesecake, and *speculoos* (SPEH-kuh-loohs), a typical crunchy gingerbread cookie popularly served with coffee. *Dame blanche* (DHAM BLAHNSJ) is another favorite made of vanilla ice cream with hot chocolate sauce poured across the top when served.

Juicy red strawberries, most famously grown at Wépion, have a special place in Belgian desserts and can be served with cream or used to decorate other desserts. Strawberries are now available through much of the year because special farms grow them in greenhouses, but the most productive strawberry season is in June and July.

Belgian chocolate is world famous. The extremely high standards and melt-in-the-mouth textures are maintained by using only 100 percent cocoa butter. In a café it is common to receive a small, individually wrapped square of chocolate with your coffee. For wrapped chocolate the most common brand is Côte d'Or. However, Belgium also has a huge number of specialist chocolate shops selling handmade, bite-size pralines (prah-LEEHN). These have a vast variety of creamy, nutty, or fruity centers. The pralines are displayed like precious items in a jewelry shop and are sold by weight. As many are made with fresh cream, they cannot be kept long, although that is seldom a problem.

A BEER TO EVERYONE'S TASTE

Beer is Belgium's national beverage. There are hundreds of brands and roughly a dozen different types of beer. Standard beers (5 percent

128

alcohol) are mostly clear lagers such as Stella Artois and unfiltered "white" beers such as the classic Hoegaarten with its hints of citrus and spice. There are also red beers, brown beers, "Scotch" beers, wheat beers, and very weak table beers. The latter have only 2 percent alcohol and were traditionally served to children with meals as a healthier alternative to sweet sodas. However, Belgium is most famous for its strong Abbey beers and other intensely flavored special brews that mostly have alcohol levels between 7 and 12 percent. For centuries monasteries were a great source of brews, and, even today, the most prized ales are made by monks. Just seven beers qualify for the prestigious label "Trappist." Of these, Chimay and Orval are the best known, but magnificently complex Westvleteren is probably the most sought after, being bottled only in tiny quantities.

Beer barrels at one of the house breweries in Belgium.

The area southwest of Brussels, called *Pajottenland* (pah-JOHT-tuhn-land), is famous for its unique self-fermenting beers called *lambik* (lahm-BEEHK). Wheat and barley are left for one night in open wooden tubs while natural fermentation starts from wild yeasts. At this stage a few wild hops that grow in the region are added. The brews are then left to mature in the barrels. The result is a golden-colored beer, but the taste is like that of astringent apple juice, so *lambiks* are usually blended to make a more palatable beer called *gueuze* (GER-z) or combined with fruit. Cherries can be added for *kriek* (creek), raspberries for *framboise* (from-BWAAZ) or, less commonly, blueberries for *myrtille* (meer-TEEy).

WATERZOOI

Serves 4

4 chicken breasts, boned and skinned
2 large boiled potatoes, peeled and cut into chunks
2 leeks, diced
3 sticks of celery, diced
2 large carrots, diced
1 large onion, diced
4 large mushrooms, diced (other vegetables can be substituted or added according to preference)
6 cups chicken stock
2 bay leaves
6 sprigs fresh parsley
4 sprigs fresh thyme
Dried tarragon to taste
1 cup heavy cream
1 teaspoon cornstarch
2 tablespoons butter
2 large egg yolks
Salt and pepper

Wash and dice the vegetables, then season them. Using a large, high-sided pot, sauté the vegetables in butter until they are slightly softened. Add the chicken stock, then bring the mixture to a boil. Add the herbs, but save two sprigs of parsely for later use as garnish. Add the chicken breasts to the boiling mix. Reduce the heat and allow the breasts to poach for around 15 minutes until tender before removing them. Strain off excess grease from the top of the broth, but do not discard the broth itself—this will be used later.

Meanwhile, mix the cream and the cornstarch together. Whisk the egg yolks (the whites are not required) and add the cream-cornstarch mix. Slowly add the mixture to the broth and stir. Add the chicken and boiled potatoes. On low heat, keep stirring while the *waterzooi* thickens somewhat, but do not overheat or the mixture will get lumpy. Add salt and pepper to taste. Remove bay leaves before serving.

Serve in four low-sided soup bowls sprinkled with the extra parsley. This rich soup, or stew, is served as a main course, usually with hot freshly baked French bread.

SUGAR TART

Serves 4

½ cup milk
½ cup white sugar
1½ ounces fresh yeast
2½ cups flour
1 sachet of vanilla sugar

3 large eggs
1 stick butter, softened
½ cup brown sugar
cream (to taste)
1 pinch of salt

Warm the milk until it is lukewarm, then combine enough of it with the white sugar, crumbled yeast, and about 3 tablespoons of the flour to make a somewhat runny mixture. Cover with a clean towel for around 15 minutes while it ferments and increases in size. Then add the rest of the flour, the vanilla sugar, and two eggs, followed by most of the butter (save a few pats), the salt and the rest of the milk. Knead the mixture gently and let it rest for at least half an hour.

Spread the dough onto a baking pan and cover it in brown sugar. Whisk the last egg and cream and smooth it evenly over the sugar. Dot with the remaining butter. Bake at 350°F (176.6°C) for 15 to 20 minutes until the brown sugar blackens into an almost burned caramel.

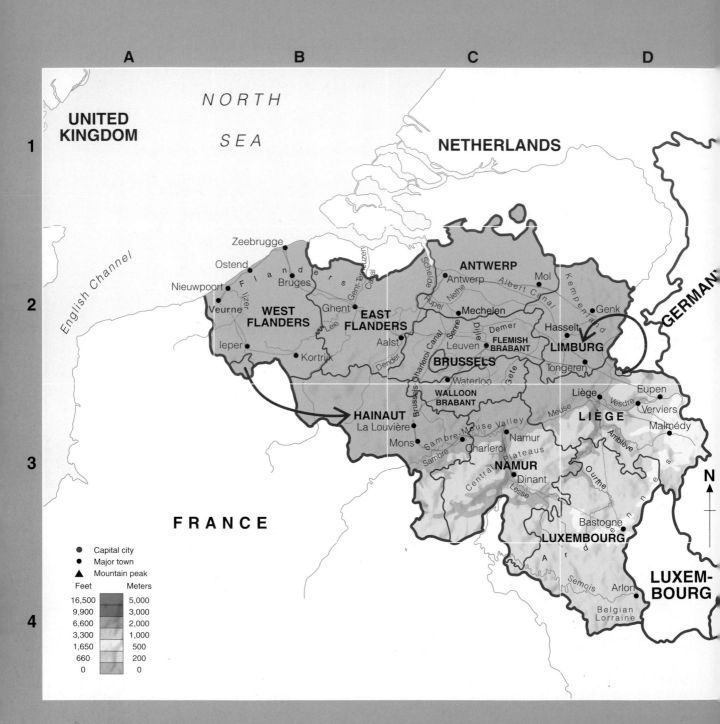

UNITED
KINGDOM

NORTH

SEA

NETHERLANDS

English Channel

Zeebrugge

Ostend

Nieuwpoort   Bruges

Veurne

WEST
FLANDERS

Ghent   EAST
             FLANDERS

Aalst

Kortrijk

Ieper

ANTWERP

Antwerp   Mol

Mechelen   Genk

Hasselt

Leuven   FLEMISH
          BRABANT   LIMBURG

BRUSSELS   Tongeren

Waterloo

WALLOON
BRABANT

HAINAUT
La Louvière

Mons   Namur

Charleroi

NAMUR
       Dinant

Liège   Eupen
             Verviers

LIÈGE   Malmédy

Bastogne

LUXEMBOURG

GERMANY

FRANCE

LUXEM-
BOURG

Arlon

Belgian
Lorraine

N

● Capital city
● Major town
▲ Mountain peak

Feet	Meters
16,500	5,000
9,900	3,000
6,600	2,000
3,300	1,000
1,650	500
660	200
0	0

MAP OF BELGIUM

Aalst, C2
Albert Canal, C2
Amblève, D3
Antwerp, C2
Ardennes, D3
Arlon, D4

Bastogne, D3
Belgian Lorraine, D4
Bruges, B2
Brussels, C2
Brussels-Charleroi Canal, C2

Central Plateaus, C3
Charleroi, C3

Demer, C2
Dender, B2, C2
Dijle, C2
Dinant, C3

East Flanders, B2, C2
English Channel, A2
Eupen, D2

Flanders, B2
Flemish Brabant, C2
France, A3,B3

Genk, D2
Ghent, B2
Ghent-Terneuzen Canal, B2
Germany, D2
Gete, C2

Hainaut, B2, B3
Hasselt, D2

Ieper, B2
Ijzer, B2

Kempenland, D2
Kortrijk, B2
La Louvière, C3

Leie, B2
Lesse, C3
Leuven, C2
Liège, D2
Limburg, D2
Luxembourg, D3
Luxembourg (Grand Duchy),
  D3, D4

Malmédy, D3
Mechelen, C2
Meuse, C3, D3
Mol, C2, D3
Mons, C3

Namur, C3
Nethe, C2
Netherlands, C1
Nieuwpoort, B2
North Sea, B1, B2

Ostend, B2
Ourthe, D3

Rupel, C2

Sambre, C3
Sambre-Meuse
Valley, C3
Schelde, C2
Semois, D3, D4
Senne, C2

Tongeren, D2

United Kingdom, A1

Verviers, D2
Vesdre, D2
Veurne, B2

Walloon Brabant, C2
Waterloo, C2
West Flanders, B2

Zeebrugge, B2

ECONOMIC BELGIUM

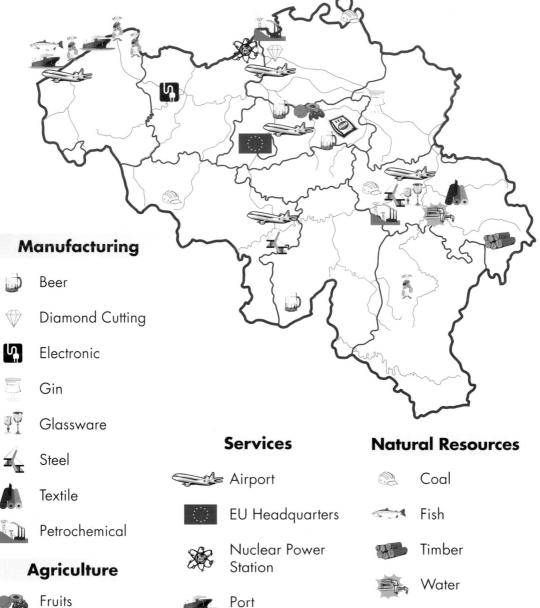

Manufacturing

- Beer
- Diamond Cutting
- Electronic
- Gin
- Glassware
- Steel
- Textile
- Petrochemical

Agriculture

- Fruits
- Sugar

Services

- Airport
- EU Headquarters
- Nuclear Power Station
- Port
- Tourism

Natural Resources

- Coal
- Fish
- Timber
- Water

ABOUT
THE ECONOMY

OVERVIEW
Belgium has an advanced and highly diversified capitalist economy. Although heavy industry still operates in the south along with major petroleum refining and the production of petrochemicals around Antwerp, the major money earners are light- and high-tech industries and, notably, service industries. Agriculture is widespread and diversified but occupies a small percentage of the population.

GROSS DOMESTIC PRODUCT (GDP)
$325 billion (2005 estimate)

GDP GROWTH
1.5 percent (2005 estimate)

GDP BY SECTOR
Agriculture 1.3 percent, industry 24.7 percent, services 74 percent (2004 estimates)

INFLATION RATE
2.7 percent (2005 estimate)

CURRENCY
Euro = 100 Euro cents
Notes: 5, 10, 20, 50, 100, 500 Euros
Coins: 1, 2 Euros; 1, 2, 5, 10, 20, 50 Euro cents
USD1 = 0.84 Euro cents (February 2006)

AGRICULTURAL PRODUCTS
Dairy, pigs, cattle, fish, crustaceans, sugar beets, potatoes, wheat, barley, hops, fruit, endive, corn

MINERAL RESOURCES
Coal (the country has coal reserves but mining has ceased), building materials, gravel

MAJOR EXPORTS
Machinery, equipment, chemicals, diamonds, metals and metal products, foodstuffs, chocolate, beer, drinking water

MAJOR IMPORTS
Machinery, equipment, chemicals, diamonds, pharmaceuticals, foodstuffs, transportation equipment, oil products

MAIN TRADE PARTNERS
Germany 19.2 percent, France 14.9 percent, Netherlands 14.2 percent, United Kingdom 7.4 percent, United States 6 percent, Ireland 5 percent (2004 estimates)

LABOR FORCE
4.77 million (2005 estimate)

LABOR FORCE BY OCCUPATION
Agriculture 13 percent, industry 24.5 percent, services 74.2 percent (2003 estimates)

UNEMPLOYMENT RATE
7.6 percent (2005 estimate)

INTERNET USERS
5.1 million (2005 estimate)

CULTURAL BELGIUM

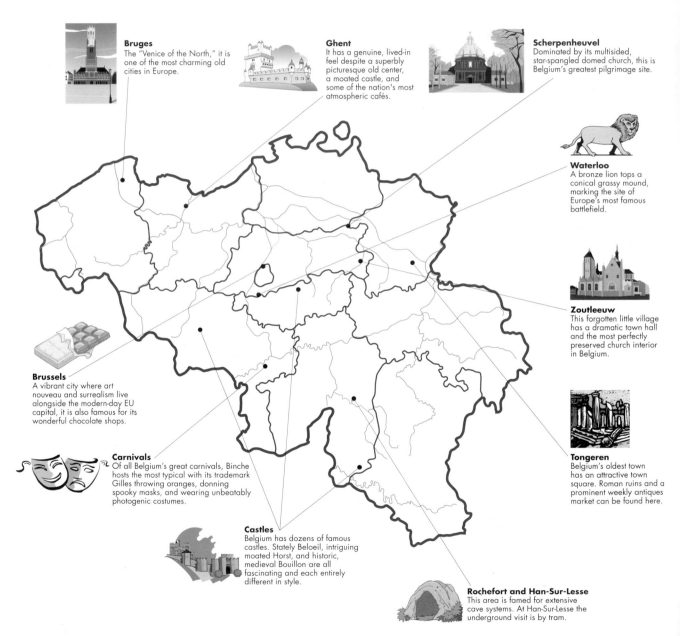

Bruges
The "Venice of the North," it is one of the most charming old cities in Europe.

Ghent
It has a genuine, lived-in feel despite a superbly picturesque old center, a moated castle, and some of the nation's most atmospheric cafés.

Scherpenheuvel
Dominated by its multisided, star-spangled domed church, this is Belgium's greatest pilgrimage site.

Waterloo
A bronze lion tops a conical grassy mound, marking the site of Europe's most famous battlefield.

Zoutleeuw
This forgotten little village has a dramatic town hall and the most perfectly preserved church interior in Belgium.

Brussels
A vibrant city where art nouveau and surrealism live alongside the modern-day EU capital, it is also famous for its wonderful chocolate shops.

Carnivals
Of all Belgium's great carnivals, Binche hosts the most typical with its trademark Gilles throwing oranges, donning spooky masks, and wearing unbeatably photogenic costumes.

Tongeren
Belgium's oldest town has an attractive town square. Roman ruins and a prominent weekly antiques market can be found here.

Castles
Belgium has dozens of famous castles. Stately Beloeil, intriguing moated Horst, and historic, medieval Bouillon are all fascinating and each entirely different in style.

Rochefort and Han-Sur-Lesse
This area is famed for extensive cave systems. At Han-Sur-Lesse the underground visit is by tram.

ABOUT THE CULTURE

OFFICIAL NAME
Kingdom of Belgium (English), Belgique (French), België (Flemish), Belgien (German)

NATIONAL FLAG
Three equal vertical stripes of black (left), yellow or gold, and red.

TOTAL AREA
11,786 square miles (30,528 square km)

CAPITAL
Brussels

POPULATION
10,379,070 (July 2006 estimate)

POPULATION GROWTH RATE
0.13 percent (2206 estimate)

ETHNO-LINGUISTIC GROUPS
Flemish 55 percent, Francophone-Belgian 32 percent, Italian-Belgian 3 percent, other (including Turkish, Moroccan, Dutch, French and German) 10 percent

MAIN LANGUAGES
Flemish, French, German (all official). English common as a second language.

MAJOR RELIGIONS
Roman Catholic, Protestant, Islam

BIRTH RATE
10.38 births per 1,000 Belgians (2006 estimate)

DEATH RATE
10.27 deaths per 1,000 Belgians (2006 estimate)

AGE DISTRIBUTION
0 to 14 years: 18 percent
15 to 59 years: 61 percent
60 years and over: 21 percent

LITERACY RATE
99 percent

NATIONAL HOLIDAYS
New Year's Day (January 1), Labor Day (May 1), Flemish Community Day (July 11, not in Wallonia), Easter Monday (dates vary), National Day (July 21), Assumption (August 15), Francophone Community Day (September 27, not in Flanders), All Saints' Day (November 1), Armistice Day (November 11), German Community Day (November 15), Christmas Day (December 25)

LEADERS IN POLITICS
King Albert II, constitutional monarch (since 1993)
Guy Verhofstadt, prime minister (since 1999)

TIME LINE

IN BELGIUM	IN THE WORLD

1500 B.C.
Celts and Franks start to settle the region.

753 B.C.
Rome is founded.

116–17 B.C.
The Roman empire reaches its greatest extent, under Emperor Trajan (98–17).

52 B.C.
Centurians defeat the Belgae tribe. The region becomes part of the Roman Empire.

A.D. 600
Height of Mayan civilization

A.D. 768–814
Reign of Charlemagne

1000
The Chinese perfect gunpowder and begin to use it in warfare.

1302
Flemish citizens defeat French knights at the Battle of the Golden Spurs.

1384–1451
The dukes of Burgundy take control.

1506
The region comes under Spanish or Hapsburg rule.

1530
Beginning of transatlantic slave trade organized by the Portuguese in Africa.

1558–1603
Reign of Elizabeth I of England

1585
Future Belgium returns to Spanish rule.

1620
Pilgrims sail the Mayflower to America.

1648
Antwerp's port is closed following the Eighty Years War (1568–1648).

1695
French forces bombard Brussels, destroying the Grand Place and stealing the Manneken Pis.

1714–94
Austrian rule

1776
U.S. Declaration of Independence

1789–99
The French Revolution

1790–92
The Brabanconne Revolution declares the United States of Belgium.

IN BELGIUM	IN THE WORLD
1795	
Belgium is annexed by revolutionary France.	
1814–30	
Belgium comes under Dutch rule.	
1815	
The Battle of Waterloo is waged.	
1830	
Belgium gains independence.	**1861**
	The U.S. Civil War begins.
	1869
1878–1908	The Suez Canal is opened.
King Leopold II develops the Congo as his own personal territory.	
1914–18	**1914**
World War I devastates western Flanders.	World War I begins.
1939–45	**1939**
World War II is waged. Belgium is occupied by Nazi Germany.	World War II begins.
	1945
	The United States drops atomic bombs on Hiroshima and Nagasaki.
	1949
	The North Atlantic Treaty Organization (NATO)
1962	is formed.
Linguistic frontier is formalized between Flemish- and French-speaking communities. Belgian Congo gains its independence.	**1966–69**
	The Chinese Cultural Revolution
1993	**1991**
The death of King Baudouin creates a brief sense of unity between linguistic regions.	Break-up of the Soviet Union
1995	
Belgium is divided into a three-part federation.	**1997**
	Hong Kong is returned to China.
1999	
Prince Philippe marries Princess Mathilde.	**2001**
2002	Terrorists crash planes in New York, Washington, D.C., and Pennsylvania.
Belgium sends troops to Afghanistan as part of the International Security Assistance Force.	
2003	**2003**
The Binche Carnival is declared a UNESCO masterpiece of intangible cultural heritage.	War in Iraq

GLOSSARY

Begijnhoven (buh-GEYEN-hoven)
Walled community of cloistered homes where women could enjoy company and security in a religious atmosphere.

craquelin (krah-kuh-LAIN)
A soft, sweet bread.

cramique (French, krah-ME-kuh)
kramiek (Flemish, krah-MEEK)
A sweet bread with currants.

duivenmelker (DEUY-vuhn-mehl-khur)
Person who breeds pigeons to race.

frieten (Flemish, FREEH-tehn)
frites (French, FREEH-tuh)
Belgian-style french fries.

Gilles (JEEH-luh)
Participants in the Binche carnival, who wear brightly colored medieval costumes. They go around town throwing oranges at the public.

La Belgitude (LAH behl-ji-TUU-duh)
Belgian art movement at the beginning of the 20th century that developed a national feeling.

Les Marolles (LEH mah-ROHL)
Old working-class area in the center of Brussels where a special dialect is spoken.

Marollien (mah-roh-LYEAN)
Typical dialect of the Marolles, a version of French mixed with Flemish words and even some Spanish.

Ommegang (OHM-muh-gang)
Historical parade held in Brussels, a reenactment of a parade held for Charles V in 1549.

polders (POHL-duhrs)
Area in Flanders Lowlands region consisting of thin, sandy soil, with clay underneath.

primeurs (pree-MEUH-rs)
Vegetables and fruits eaten at the very beginning of their season.

speculoos (SPEH-kuh-loohs)
Crunchy gingerbread cookies.

taalvrijheid (TAAHL-vreye-heyet)
The right to use Flemish as an official language, claimed by the Flemings.

tarte al d'jote (TARHT ahl DJOH-tuh)
Typical Walloon flan made of beet leaves and cheese.

Walloon (wah-LOHN)
Group of French dialects spoken in Wallonia, with origins in the old Celtic and Germanic languages.

waterzooi (WAH-tuhr-zoohj)
Typical Flemish dish, made of fish or chicken in a soup with potatoes, carrots, leeks, and cream.

witloof (WHIT-loohf)
Belgian endive, a form of chicory bud, that is a popular white vegetable used in salad or cooked.

FURTHER INFORMATION

BOOKS

Adkin, Mark. *The Waterloo Companion*. London: Aurum Press, 2001.

Aronson, Theo. *The Coburgs of Belgium*. London: Cassell, 1968.

Blom, J. C. H. and Lambert, E. *History of the Low Countries*. Oxford: Berghahn Books, 1999.

Deglas, Christian. *Le Goût de la Bière Belge*. Braine-l'Alleud, Belgium: Editions J-M Collet, 1995.

Elliott, Mark. *Culture Shock! Belgium*. London: Kuperard, 2002.

Van Waerebeek-Gonzalez, Ruth. *Everybody Eats Well in Belgium Cookbook*. New York: Workman Publishing, 1996.

Wickman, Stephen B. *Belgium, A Country Study*. Washington, D.C.: U.S. Government Printing Office, 1985.

WEB SITES

BBC News. www.news.bbc.co.uk

Belgian Government Statistical Office. http://statbel.fgov.be/home_fr.asp

Belgian Natural Parks. http://birdlist.org/eur/belgie/be_parks.htm

CIA Factbook. www.cia.gov/cia/publications/factbook/geos/be.html

Flanders Online. www.flanders.be

Flemish Tourist Office. www.visitflanders.com

Organisation for Economic Co-operation and Development. www.oecd.org

Wallonia Online. www.wallonie.be

BIBLIOGRAPHY

Adkin, Mark. *The Waterloo Companion*. London: Aurum Press, 2001.

Aronson, Theo. *The Coburgs of Belgium*. London: Cassell, 1968.

Belgopocket. Available free from Belgian post offices and updated every year.

Blom, J. C. H. and Lambert, E. *History of the Low Countries*. Oxford: Berghahn Books, 1999.

Deglas, Christian. *Le Gout de la Bière Belge*. Braine-l'Alleud, Belgium: Editions J-M Collet, 1995.

Elliott, Mark. *Culture Shock! Belgium*. London: Kuperard, 2002.

Lerner Publications. *Belgium in Pictures*. Minneapolis, MN: Lerner Publications, 1991.

Parker, Geoffrey. *The Dutch Revolt*. London: Penguin, 1990.